Keeping the Leadership in Instructional Leadership

In a high-stakes and testing-focused school climate, principals strive to develop and refine the skills that will make them effective instructional leaders. This book discusses how a narrow focus on day-to-day operations and management can limit the potential for effective instructional leadership by drawing attention away from the behaviors and interpersonal skills that enable school administrators to succeed. Building on stories from experienced principals in school districts across the country, author Linda L. Carrier offers practical tips and strategies for restoring the human dynamic of instructional leadership. *Keeping the Leadership in Instructional Leadership: Developing Your Practice* is designed to facilitate personal reflection and conversation about leadership practice, and its advice will empower principals and administrators to transform their schools into highly engaged communities of learners.

Linda L. Carrier, Ed.D., is Assistant Professor of Educational Leadership and Graduate Program Advisor at Plymouth State University, USA.

Other Eye On Education Books
Available from Routledge
(www.routledge.com/eyeoneducation)

Ten Steps for Genuine Leadership in Schools
David M. Fultz

College for Every Student: A Practitioner's Guide to Building College and Career Readiness
Rick Dalton and Edward P. St. John

Leading Learning for ELL Students: Strategies for Success
Catherine Beck and Heidi Pace

Leadership in America's Best Urban Schools
Joseph F. Johnson, Jr., Cynthia L. Uline, and Lynne G. Perez

The Power of Conversation: Transforming Principals into Great Leaders
Barbara Kohm

First Aid for Teacher Burnout: How You Can Find Peace and Success
Jenny G. Rankin

What Successful Principals Do! 199 Tips for Principals, 2nd Edition
Franzy Fleck

The Revitalized Tutoring Center: A Guide to Transforming School Culture
Jeremy Koselak and Brad Lyall

7 Ways to Transform the Lives of Wounded Students
Joe Hendershott

School Leadership Through the Seasons: A Guide to Staying Focused and Getting Results All Year
Ann T. Mausbach and Kimberly Morrison

Distributed Leadership in Schools: A Practical Guide for Learning and Improvement
John A. DeFlaminis, Mustafa Abdul-Jabbar, and Eric Yoak

The Leader's Guide to Working with Underperforming Teachers: Overcoming Marginal Teaching and Getting Results
Sally Zepeda

Five Critical Leadership Practices: The Secret to High-Performing Schools
Ruth C. Ash and Pat H. Hodge

Strategies for Developing and Supporting School Leaders: Stepping Stones to Great Leadership
Karen L. Sanzo

Keeping the Leadership in Instructional Leadership

Developing Your Practice

Linda L. Carrier

Routledge
Taylor & Francis Group
NEW YORK AND LONDON

First published 2017
by Routledge
711 Third Avenue, New York, NY 10017

and by Routledge
2 Park Square, Milton Park, Abingdon, Oxon, OX14 4RN

Routledge is an imprint of the Taylor & Francis Group, an informa business

© 2017 Taylor & Francis

The right of Linda L. Carrier to be identified as the author of this work has been asserted by her in accordance with sections 77 and 78 of the Copyright, Designs and Patents Act 1988.

All rights reserved. No part of this book may be reprinted or reproduced or utilised in any form or by any electronic, mechanical, or other means, now known or hereafter invented, including photocopying and recording, or in any information storage or retrieval system, without permission in writing from the publishers.

Trademark notice: Product or corporate names may be trademarks or registered trademarks, and are used only for identification and explanation without intent to infringe.

Library of Congress Cataloging in Publication Data
A catalog entry of this book has been requested

ISBN: 978-1-138-95779-4 (hbk)
ISBN: 978-1-138-95780-0 (pbk)
ISBN: 978-1-315-66152-0 (ebk)

Typeset in Optima
by Florence Production Ltd, Stoodleigh, Devon, UK

To my children, Josh, Zac, and Sam, and my granddaughter Lily.
Find your passion and pursue it every day.
Give yourselves time. Nothing worth accomplishing happens overnight.
Love what you do every day.
Enthusiastically learn all you can about what you love doing.
Endeavor to pursue your passion honestly and with integrity.

> "Dream lofty dreams, and as you dream, so shall you become.
> Your Vision is the promise of what you shall one day be.
> Your Ideal is the prophecy of what you shall at last unveil."
> — James Allen

Contents

Meet the Author ix
Preface xi

1. **The Challenge of Instructional Leadership** 1
   The School Principal 3
   Redefining the Focus of Principals: Standards-Based Reform 4
   The Journey to Instructional Leadership 5
   To Be or Not to Be: The Moral Purpose 10
   Questions for Reflection and Discussion 13

2. **The Practice of Instructional Leadership** 17
   Management Versus Leadership 19
   The Practice of Instructional Leadership: An Introduction 26
   Instructional 27
   Focused on Learning 28
   High Expectations 29
   Data-Based Decision Making 30
   Developing Communities Around a Single Vision and Mission 32
   No One Way 33
   Leadership 34
   Questions for Reflection and Discussion 35

3. **The Work of the Principal** 39
   Focuses on Learning 39
   Communicates High Expectations 45
   Data-Based Decision Making 48

Contents

    Facilitates a Unified Vision and Mission 51
    No Two Alike 56
    Questions for Reflection and Discussion 57

4. **The Leadership of the Principal**   59
    Authentic to Self 61
    Fearlessness 65
    Personally Humble and Modest 69
    How Can I Develop My Leadership? 70
    Mindfulness 71
    Personal Reflection 74
    Coaching 77
    Questions for Reflection and Discussion 79

5. **Overcoming Perceived Barriers**   82
    Personal Vision and Mission 82
    Potential Barriers to Developing a Holistic Practice of
        Instructional Leadership 85
    The New England Models 92
    Community Conformity 95
    Questions for Reflection and Discussion 100

6. **Keeping the Leadership in Your Practice**   104
    Advocating for Effective Practice 105
    Developing District Level Support for Instructional
        Leadership 106
    Educating and Working with Policy-Makers 108
    Working with Institutes of Higher Education and Professional
        Development Providers 109
    Pausing the Conversation 111
    Questions for Reflection and Discussion 111

Meet the Author

Currently Assistant Professor of Educational Leadership at Plymouth State University, Linda Carrier began her career in education as an elementary and middle level music educator in a large urban school district in Western, Massachusetts. She has served as an elementary, middle, and K-8 school principal in both urban and suburban school districts in the Commonwealth, also working as a central office administrator providing leadership for curriculum and instruction in both suburban and rural districts.

Entering into her work in middle school during the early stage of implementation of the Massachusetts Education Reform Act of 1993, she saw the need for a new way of leading schools and of principals engaging in their roles. Developing her own professional practice to provide instructional leadership in schools, Linda dedicated her career in school leadership to leading schools that had been identified as underperforming. Together with teachers she was able to meet her personal mission of creating the type of schools she wanted for her own children. Combining her passion for that work with her work in higher education, she now teaches the next generation of principals, superintendents, and curriculum administrators and continues to pursue her passion for school leadership through studying the practices of school leaders.

Preface

What This Book is About

The research is abundant and clear, effective leadership of schools is necessary for improved student achievement. Both the research and policy agenda of the last twenty years has also been clear; to be an effective school leader in the age of standards and high-stakes accountability specifically means being an instructional leader. But what *is* instructional leadership? The term and its implications seem simple. Perhaps more importantly, *what does it look like in practice when it is implemented effectively?* Through my personal experience as a school administrator in Western Massachusetts, my practice as an Assistant Professor of Educational Leadership, and my research in the field it has become clear to me that what some assume is a straight forward clear idea may in fact be cast in shadows of uncertainty and misunderstanding. A phenomenon rooted in the myopic focus of policy-makers, researchers, and subsequently the field on the *tasks* of instructional leadership. Written as a guide, *Keeping the Leadership in Instructional Leadership: Developing Your Practice* provides answers to what instructional leadership is and supports readers in developing their vision of what it can look like in their own practice.

Who This Book is For

Certainly, the continued widespread identification of low-performing and failing schools would suggest that there are a large number of principals that may not be implementing an effective model of instructional leadership. Still others are implementing strong instructional leadership practices but

Preface

because the level of student achievement doesn't match prescribed benchmarks feel and are often given feedback they are not. Regardless of what you currently believe or perhaps are being told about your practice, *Keeping the Leadership in Instructional Leadership: Developing Your Practice* has been written for you. Developed to assist school principals in reflecting on their personal practice by exploring the issues of what effective instructional leadership looks like, why leadership may be being left behind in the practice, and the need to focus not only on the tasks instructional leaders do but also the leadership they provide. The stories of two turn around principals from Massachusetts, National Association of Elementary School Principals National Distinguished Principals (NDPs), my own, and other principals in the field will be used to bring the issues and practice to life.

How This Book is Organized

In order to guide readers in reflecting on and developing their own practices, *Keeping the Leadership in Instructional Leadership: Developing Your Practice* has been organized through six chapters, each designed to address a particular issue to be considered and to build on those previous. Beginning with developing common language and background knowledge, Chapters 1 and 2 introduce the concept of instructional leadership and why we as school leaders strive to become instructional leaders. Moving more deeply into the concept of instructional leadership, Chapters 3 and 4 examine the *work* of instructional leaders and their *leadership*. The final two chapters, 5 and 6, have been written to both support you in considering the various barriers that you may encounter while trying to develop your practice and how you can begin to develop your practice in the way you envision.

Special Features

Instead of providing a "how to" guide this book draws on research, mine and others, and the stories of principals who have been identified as instructional leaders to engage readers in reflection and professional discourse about their professional practice. *Keeping the Leadership in Instructional Leadership: Developing Your Practice* uses *Voices from*

Leaders in the Field and *Questions for Reflection and Discussion* to support that process. Provided through the *Voices from Leaders in the Field* feature, the stories principals provide insights and examples of instructional leadership in practice. Combined with a feature called *Questions for Reflection and Discussion* the sharing of these stories is not meant to provide a directive for the practice of instructional leadership but rather to provide a point to begin personal reflection and conversation about the practice so that we each may develop our own and so that we as a profession may grow.

The Challenge of Instructional Leadership

Instructional leadership—it's something all educators hear about and all school principals are told they should practice. Over the last twenty years the expectation for the role of school principals has changed from that of a business management model to one that is focused on student achievement. Principals across the country strive every day to develop the skills and practices that they believe will make them effective school leaders in the current educational environment; specifically those that will make them instructional leaders. While some principals have been recognized for their practices, others continue to try and unlock what they perceive as the mystery of instructional leadership. The fact they are *doing* all the things they believe instructional leaders do and not achieving the desired results in student achievement has created the mystique of the practice. Perhaps you're asking yourself, "What is it that these principals are doing that I'm missing?" Or, "I'm doing what I should be, why isn't it working?" As we begin to understand the answers to these questions, we must first understand—why do we want to become instructional leaders anyway?

Throughout the history of America's public education system the message has been communicated that America's public schools are failing. Regardless of one's personal belief in that message, it has too often become a battle cry in our country that is renewed with each presidential election cycle. With each volley of criticisms a new set of expectations for schools and educators emerges; mandating changes in the breadth of educational practice through reform policies. Although as a profession we try to keep up with what has become rapid waves of reform, as individuals we often are unclear if we're being successful in our attempts to meet the demands.

Amid the modern era of widespread educational reform, multiple constituencies and stakeholders have sought to develop solutions to America's perceived public school shortcomings. Researchers, policy-makers, and K-12 educators have independently and collectively sought to ask and respond to the points of urgency and host of questions and answers, identified by legislation like *A Nation at Risk* (1983), the No Child Left Behind Act (NCLB) (2001), and the Race to the Top Act (RttT) (2009) of *failing schools* in America. As a result of the questions and concerns posed by the authors of these documents, state-level policy-makers have answered the call-to-arms demanded by their constituencies by developing policies that they believe will improve America's schools. A significant part of these policy initiatives during the last twenty years has been the identification of *underperforming* schools, sanctions for underperformance, and the implementation of state intervention strategies for improving identified schools (Anderson & Lewis, 1997; DiMaggio, 2003; Krueger, Snow-Renner, & Ziebarth, 2002; Mintrop, MacLellan, & Quintero, 2001; Seder, 2000).

As a result of NCLB legislation, American educators were for the first time in their history being asked to measure their success as educators against their students' academic performance, a practice they were largely unprepared to undertake (Elmore, 2002; Lashway, 2002; Leithwood & Riehl, 2003; National Association of Elementary School Principals, 2001; Waters, Marzano, & McNulty, 2003). Significant to this legislation and a landmark in the history of federal education legislation was the penalty for low student academic performance in the way of prescribed state sanctions. Among the more notable of the sanctions was the provision of school choice for students attending underperforming schools, mandated use of federal Title 1 funds for supplemental educational services, and the removal of school staff (Anderson & Lewis, 1997; DiMaggio, 2003; Duffy, 2001; Krueger *et al.*, 2002; Mintrop *et al.*, 2001; No Child Left Behind, 2001; Seder, 2000).

You may be asking what the implications of the policy stream have been for the role of school principal. Perhaps you're asking if it has changed the expectations of the position. Or perhaps you're asking how the practices of principals have changed in response to the policy stream. Perhaps you don't accept that policy should define your practice and you're simply interested in what school principals do that makes the most impact on student achievement. In order to begin to understand the answers to those questions we must first have a common understanding of the principalship.

The School Principal

The role of the school principal has long been considered to be an important component in the process of schooling (Hallinger & Heck, 1998; Quinn, 2002; Waters, Marzano, & McNulty, 2003). Three groups of researchers—Leithwood and Riehl (2003), Waters, Marzano, and McNulty (2003), and Hallinger and Heck (1998)—conducted reviews of the existing body of research on the relationship between principal leadership and student achievement. Through their analyses of literature, these groups of researchers confirmed that the leadership of the school principal influences student achievement.

Hallinger and Heck (1998) examined research that was conducted between 1980 and 1995 on the contribution of principals to school effectiveness. In order to be included in their review, studies needed to clearly conceptualize and measure principal leadership as an independent variable and to explicitly measure school performance as a dependent variable. As a result of their analysis of the selected research, they concluded that principals have an indirect effect on student achievement. They additionally found that those studies that were classified through the Mediated-Effects Models most consistently yielded results that indicated evidence of positive effects on student achievement as a result of principal leadership behaviors.

In 2003, Leithwood and Riehl conducted an analysis of research that focused on formal building-level leadership. As a result of their analysis, they concluded that the concept of leadership includes two main functions: to "provide direction and exercise influence" (p. 7). Additionally, through their review, they found agreement with Hallinger and Heck's earlier work—that school leadership, as it works through the school's mission, goals, curriculum, and instructional practice, has an indirect impact on student achievement that is possible to be verified. In the same year, Waters, Marzano, and McNulty published their own analysis of the research. Focusing on the effects of the leadership practices of principals on student achievement, their analysis supported the findings of the other studies of this kind, that is that a "substantial relationship between leadership and student achievement exists" (p. 3).

What we also know through research is that effective leadership is essential to the development of both the organizational capacity and coherence that are necessary to effectively implement improvement initiatives in schools (Andrews & Soder, 1987; Carrier, 2011; Elmore, 2000, 2002; Hallinger & Heck, 1998; King, 2002; Krueger et al., 2002; National Association of Elementary School Principals, 2001; Newman, King, & Rigdon, 1997; Waters et al., 2003). The education reform policies of the late 20th and early 21st centuries included structures that not only provided evidence of the research base but of a public belief that the leadership of our schools is significant to our children's future. These structures included the removal of principals of chronically underperforming schools (NCLB, 2001), substantial professional development efforts for school principals (RttT, 2009), and the inclusion of student achievement data as a measure of principal effectiveness (USDOE, 2012). Although grounded in the belief that effective leadership is essential to effective schools, NCLB and RttT did not meet their stated goals and we continue as a country to struggle with issues of literacy, numeracy, and high school drop-out rates. The implementation of ESEA waivers in 2012 mandated a new model for evaluating the effectiveness of educators by formally including the use of student achievement data as an element of the process (USDOE, 2012). If we accept this *new* model for evaluating educators, which includes the evaluation of school principals as a valid means of determining the effectiveness of principals, then it stands to reason that, as a country we will have finally solved the issue of low student achievement. If, however, we believe that the effectiveness of principals is a richer deeper construct than student achievement data and other tangible sources of information can reliably and validly measure, then the question remains *"What is effective leadership in American public schools and what does it look like in practice?"*

Redefining the Focus of Principals: Standards-Based Reform

In order to begin to understand what effective leadership is in American public schools for the 21st century, we must first acknowledge a significant new element that entered into the educational paradigm over the last twenty years—state and national curriculum standards. Premised on the idea that school systems, schools, and educators should be held accountable for student outcomes, the standards-based reform movement began to shift the focus of principals away from the business management model to one that was academically focused (Elmore, 2000; Hopkins & Reynolds, 2001).

The standards-based reforms of the late 1990s and early 2000s included strong accountability measures and requirements for addressing persistent low performance, yet schools continued to be identified as underperforming. Krueger and his colleagues (2002) argued that high-stakes accountability is an insufficient means to increase student achievement and offered that, in order to be an effective piece of the reform puzzle, it must function in tandem with strong organizational capacity.

Commonly defined through budget, organizational capacity was simply defined by O'Day, Goertz, and Floden (1995) as the ability of a system to achieve its mission. Clearly that is the essence of organizational capacity, but looking more deeply at the construct, it is the degree to which a given set of ingredients relates to each other to achieve the mission of the system that makes the difference between an organization having strong organizational capacity or not (Elmore, 2002; Krueger et al., 2002; Newman et al., 1997). Although the elements of financial, human, and material resources are inherent to the various definitions, what is critical is the necessity that these elements synergistically relate to each other. In the case of schools, this synergy, commonly referred to as organizational coherence, must intentionally be influenced, finessed, and nurtured through the care of a principal with the vision and will to do so.

The Journey to Instructional Leadership

Over the course of the last twenty years a common understanding has emerged that the standards movement in education necessarily requires principals to be instructional leaders (Elmore, 2000; Fink & Resnick, 1999; King, 2002; NAESP, 2001). In 2000, Richard Elmore identified instructional leadership as "the equivalent of the holy grail in educational administration" (p. 7). King (2002) further mystified the construct by pointing out there is "no litmus test for its presence" (p. 63). In 2001, the Commonwealth of Massachusetts declared its first two schools as underperforming as a result of persistent low performance on state testing. The onset of this stage in the Commonwealth's educational reform history also marked the beginning of a formal shift in the expectation for school principals to be instructional leaders.

I was appointed to my first administrative experience, assistant principal, at one of those schools. The school was an urban middle school in the poorest city in the state. A key finding of the state's analysis of the school's professional practices was that it lacked in instructional leadership. In collaboration with the building principal and my co-assistant principal, we set out in that first year to understand what was expected of us as *instructional leaders*. What should we be doing? How should we be doing it? As part of the state's intervention into the school we were provided with reform partners whose mission was to assist us with developing our administrative practices so that we could act as change agents for improving test scores—so that we could become instructional leaders. Developing our administrative practices in this model meant making sure *our teachers were doing their jobs*. School improvement was a top down process. Of no surprise to readers, scores did not improve as a result of this model. In fact, they remained flat and more importantly the climate of the school became negative. Teachers felt they were continually under attack and as their feelings of competence eroded, so too did school climate. As reform in the state continued to unfold, more and more schools were identified as underperforming and more and more school administrators were told they needed to become instructional leaders. As we attended a variety of training, conferences, and meetings that were required by virtue of our underperforming status, we were part of more and more conversations that sought to answer the question, *what exactly is it that they are asking us to do?*

As I moved into my first principalship and my practice as a principal developed, I found that I was talking more and more *with* teachers about why they made instructional choices and how they designed instruction. Again, charged with *turning around* a persistently underperforming urban school, we began to look together as a faculty at various sources of data and together made thoughtful decisions about what to do in response. Together we took action to address the issues with student learning we were identifying. Although we knew our success would be evaluated by the district superintendent and state department of education through student achievement on the state test, we chose to focus on what our kids needed as learners.

The evaluation of teachers, contrary to the district paradigm, was an opportunity for professional growth and we engaged together as professionals in examining instructional practices for the purpose of developing so that we could better serve our students. While state test scores may not have risen to the levels required by the state to come off the underperforming list, we did see improvement on that measure and the others we had been considering. More importantly, the level of instruction improved and the shared commitment to student achievement was palpable. Our professional culture was vibrant, healthy, and deeply committed to developing our professional practices. But yet, the message continued to come from the central office and the state department of education that we, my assistant principal and I, needed to become instructional leaders. We continued to work with reform partners and attend professional development opportunities, both mandated and not, and continued to find ourselves in conversations with other passionate committed school administrators who were also struggling to understand what was being asked of them.

In 2008, I interviewed two principals of schools that had been declared models of professional practice by the Commonwealth of Massachusetts. As part of that process each of the principals was explicitly identified as an instructional leader. What was interesting about these two principals is that each had been the principal of the school for over ten years, each was leading an urban school, and each had led their school from persistently underperforming to their current status as exemplars. Surely they would have the answer to the questions my colleagues and I had been asking since 2001. During my time with them I asked them each about how their practice changed relative to the turnaround of their schools.

The first of the two, we'll call her "Lisa", had been at the helm of her small urban elementary school for nineteen years. Her 160-student school had an extremely diverse socioeconomic community and a staff of eighteen teachers. After a discussion about the message that was consistently delivered to principals of underperforming schools that they become instructional leaders, I asked Lisa what changed about her practice that resulted in the turnaround of the school. What she shared surprised, confused, and delighted me.

> The reality is I've always been an instructional leader. That's just who I am. That's just where I am. Whether it said it on paper or not that's what I was doing. Part of it was the realization on my part that what I'm good at and like to do best is work with kids and teachers.

The second of the principals, we'll call him "Terry", was principal of a much larger urban elementary school, he had also been the leader of his school for nineteen years. The 718-student school was predominantly low income and made up of students whose first language was not English. The school had seventy teachers and, due to district organization of services, the majority of the students were bussed from other less affluent neighborhoods into the middle-class neighborhood in which the school was located in the city. When I asked him about how his practice had changed he reflected on the National Institute for School Leadership (NISL) training he was participating in at the time.

> Getting back to NISL training . . . they really tell you a lot about instructional leadership and what you should be doing as a principal but this place is huge. I've got 700 kids and seventy teachers. I just can't work the way they say I should. I can't be in classrooms all day and spending time coaching. Again, I'm just lucky I've got good people. They saw what we needed to do, I got them the things they said they needed, and they did it. That really helped me to be able to manage all this—run the building I mean.

Clearly the two principals had slightly different philosophies about what instructional leadership was and how it was practiced, and neither had changed their practice in order to turnaround their schools. Then what was it that made the difference in these schools? What was it that made these two principals instructional leaders? What was obvious in my conversation with them is that neither viewed student test scores as evidence of the existence of instructional leadership and that neither viewed instructional leadership as a to-do list. It was clear to me in my conversations with them that instructional leadership was in many ways a personal journey: a journey defined by our personal vision and mission and the needs of our schools.

In 2014, I had the opportunity to present at the annual conference of the National Association of Elementary School Principals. There to discuss the idea of putting the leadership back into the practice of instructional leadership, I posed the question to the audience, "How many of you feel you are instructional leaders?" Of the forty participants in the audience, a quarter responded they believed they were not or that they were unsure if they were instructional leaders. During our conversation I was reminded of the beginnings of my own career as a school leader. Many in the audience shared stories of their frustration and concern with wanting to become an instructional leader but feeling like they continually fell short because test scores didn't reach defined levels. It was clear from the group that they felt their level of instructional leadership practice was defined by test scores; and subsequently so was their professional, and in some cases personal, value.

As part of our conversation I posed the question to the group, "What do you believe instructional leaders do?" Their responses broke into two broad categories: those related to instructional practices and those reflective of the leadership and supervisory role of the principal. Of the 76 percent that related to instructional practice, 63 percent reflected that the group believed instructional leaders provide instructional coaching, while 18.5 percent of that group believed instructional leaders evaluate instruction, and the remaining 18.5 percent believed they empower teachers to do their job. Examination of the responses that were reflective of the supervisory and leadership role of the principal reveal that 57 percent of that category could be described as management functions (i.e., maintain a focus on the

Table 1.1 What Do You Believe Instructional Leaders Do? (N = 40)

Instructional Practices	**76%**
Empowering teachers to do their jobs	18.5%
Evaluating teachers and ensuring high quality teaching	18.5%

Instructional coaching:
    Assisting in improving instruction
    Providing actionable feedback
    Learning from and with teachers
    Conferencing
    Modeling
	63%

Leadership and Supervisory Practices	**24%**

Management functions:
    Maintain a focus on the mission
    Use data
    Ensure high quality education
	57%

Leadership behaviors:
    Develop leadership
    Inspire
	43%

mission, use data) while 43 percent could be described as leadership-type behaviors (i.e., inspire, develop leaders). While the data generated from the question did not surprise me, it was reminiscent of those early days of my administration career and the things that concerned me. Had we as a profession truly not developed our understanding of instructional leadership over the last thirteen years? Could it be that we were still sending principals flawed messages about what an instructional leader does in practice?

As I work and speak with principals across the country I am struck by how many are still working from the more traditional business model of school leadership (Tyack & Cuban, 1995) and the variety of reasons for which they do so. While this book is dedicated to exploring what instructional leadership looks like in the practice of principals, I feel it necessary to first establish why, beyond policy demands, I personally believe principals should be instructional leaders.

To Be or Not to Be: The Moral Purpose

If we, as educators, accept the current policies that have emerged as a result of the ability of states to obtain waivers from the requirements of the Elementary and Secondary Education Act of 2001 (ESEA)—more commonly known today as the No Child Left Behind Act (NCLB)—to measure professional performance against student academic performance, then we must also acknowledge a compelling need to continually improve our knowledge and skills in a way that renders our professional practices as educators more effective in that context. Much like the logic behind most ethical dilemmas, we must ask, "What if we don't agree with those polices?" As school principals charged with ensuring that all learners in our care are well prepared to participate in life beyond the schoolhouse, we must also develop our practices as educators to be more effective simply because we have a moral purpose by virtue of our charge to do so.

Unfortunately, for today's school leaders, meeting the challenges of this moral purpose often means taking on tasks and responsibilities that they are unprepared to assume (Elmore, 2000; Waters et al., 2003). The uncertainty is made more complex through a lack of clarity around a standard definition of the construct of instructional leadership (King, 2002; Quinn, 2002; Waters et al., 2003). As a result of this uncertainty, many principals with whom I speak share a sense of inadequacy and question their personal level of competency. Not uncommonly they share feelings of hopelessness that they *can* be instructional leaders.

As a result of the rapidly changing and prescriptive policy environment, principals everywhere in this country are faced with a landslide of demands that take them away from the time needed to engage in the instructional leadership of schools. The frenzied rush to check off a prescribed number of walk-throughs, the demand to spend a given amount of hours in classrooms each day, short employment contracts, accountability issues, and initiative overload have robbed our schools of the precious resource of the leadership these passionate people enter their offices with every day. Over and over I hear from principals who are disheartened by the trend. They feel their ability to engage in matters of the heart and to develop authentic and caring relationships with those they lead has been substantially minimized if not eliminated by the need to accomplish a checklist of tasks. They believe their ability to authentically and meaningfully deal with the very personal element of leadership has been taken from them. The intention of the policies creating these issues is to raise student achievement. The unintended consequence is that *the practice of leadership* is being eroded in schools everywhere in our country and being substituted by the continued practice of a management model, a model that can only offer us assurance that compliance with policy demands will be met. This model will not and has not served our children well.

For principals struggling with these questions, take heart. That you are asking the questions is the first step in developing your practice, and the ability to become an instructional leader is possible. *Keeping the Leadership in Instructional Leadership* has been written to assist you with asking and answering the questions of how to develop and nourish your instructional leadership practice. What is instructional leadership? What does it look like in practice? How is policy defining the practice of instructional leadership? And finally, how do we put and keep leadership in our practice as instructional leaders? Brought to life through the experiences of school principals who have led schools from being deemed underperforming to high-performing, National Distinguished Principals of the Year, other principals in the field, and my own personal experience as a principal in Massachusetts that led schools to improve student achievement, we will explore and answer these questions.

Before we continue with our exploration let's first meet our eight exemplar principals. Pseudonyms have been used in all cases in order to protect the privacy of the principals and their teachers, and to ensure them the ability to speak freely and openly about their experience.

- "Bonnie" had twelve years of teaching experience in middle-level classrooms before moving into an administrative role in a large urban middle school. During her time in the classroom she earned the distinction of Teacher of Year in the large urban district she worked in. At the time she was awarded the National Distinguished Principal honor (2013) she had been in the role of assistant or principal in the same school for six years. During that time she led the school through a substantial transformation that resulted in marked gains in student achievement.
- "Bob" is the principal of a grade 9–12 high school in a relatively affluent suburban area. Prior to that he had served in leadership and teaching capacities in other high schools in his region. Presented with the opportunity to build a school from the ground up, Bob facilitated the development of a high school program that is focused on providing learning experiences that will prepare students for their future in the 21st century.
- Entering the field of education as a second career, "Doug" taught for three years before moving into the role of school leader. First serving as an assistant principal in a large urban elementary school, Doug had been in his role of principal for six years when he was honored as a National Distinguished Principal in 2014. As the principal of a small rural pre-K-6 elementary school in a moderately geographically isolated area, Doug has been able to lead his school to consistently being rated as a top achieving school in his state.
- "Helen," a very experienced veteran educator, served as third grade teacher for twelve years before moving into school administration. At the time she was awarded the National Distinguished Principal distinction (2014) she had served in her current school as the assistant principal for nine years and the principal for five. During that time she led her suburban 400 student grade 3–5 elementary school from being underperforming to earning several recognitions for student achievement.
- "Larry" has served as the principal of his large urban grade 9–12 high school for ten years. Prior to that he served as its assistant principal and taught history in a neighboring high school. Leading his school from the stereotypical hierarchical compartmentalized high school model

to one that is based on collaboration, distributed leadership, and curriculum integration, Larry's reputation, as an instructional leader is well known in his region.

- "Lisa" had been at the helm of her small 120 student urban elementary school for nineteen years when her state identified her as an instructional leader and an exemplar. Having led her 160-student urban K-5 elementary school from being chronically underperforming to exemplary, Lisa's work as an instructional leader gained recognition and awareness through her state's accountability system.

- "Penny" had been in the role of principal in her 500 student suburban middle school for five years when she was identified as a National Distinguished Principal in 2013. Prior to that she served as an assistant principal and classroom teacher in a neighboring middle school. Committed to middle-level philosophy, Penny has led her school through the high-stakes accountability movement without sacrificing the hallmarks of middle-level education.

- "Terry" is the principal of a large urban K-5 elementary school. His school of 718 students is predominantly low income and includes a high percentage of students for whom English is not their first language. Under Terry's leadership the school moved from being identified as chronically underperforming to being exemplary. Like Lisa, Terry had been the leader of his school for nineteen years when his state identified him as an exemplar instructional leader for his work in turning the school around.

Questions for Reflection and Discussion

1. Why do you want to be an instructional leader?
2. What do you believe instructional leaders do?
3. Why do you currently believe you are, or are not, an instructional leader?
4. What do you believe has contributed to or influenced your current instructional leadership practice?
5. Reflect on a school principal, other than yourself, that you believe is an instructional leader. How do you believe their practice varies for your own?

References

Anderson, A.B. and Lewis, A.C. (1997). *Academic Bankruptcy*. Denver, CO: Education Commission of the States.

Andrews, R. and Soder, R. (1987). Principal leadership and student achievement. *Educational Leadership*, 44(6), 9–11.

Carrier, L. (2011). *What is instructional leadership and what does it look like in practice? A multi-case case study of elementary school principals who have led schools from being identified as underperforming to performing*. Doctoral Dissertation. Amherst, MA: University of Massachusetts.

DiMaggio, M. (2003). State support to low-performing schools. Washington, DC: The Chief State School Officers. Retrieved on February 18, 2004 from www.ecs.org.

Duffy, M. (2001). *America's reform inferno: The nine layers of accountability*. Paper presented at the annual meeting of the American Educational Research Association. Seattle, WA.

Elmore, R. (2000). *Building a New Structure for School Leadership*. Washington, DC: Albert Shanker Institute.

Elmore, R. (2002). Bridging the Gap between Standards and Achievement. Washington, DC: Albert Shanker Institute.

Fink, E. and Resnick, L. (1999). Developing principals as instructional leaders. Pittsburgh High Performance Learning Communities Project, Learning Research and Development Center. Pittsburgh, PA: University of Pittsburgh. Retrieved on September 17, 2007 from www.lrdc.pitt.edu/hplc.

Hallinger, P. and Heck, R. (1998). Exploring the principal's contribution to school effectiveness: 1980–1995. *School Effectiveness and School Improvement*, 9(2), 157–191.

Hopkins, D. and Reynolds, D. (2001). The past, present and future of school improvement: Towards the third age. *British Educational Research Journal*, 27(4), 459–475.

King, D. (2002). The changing shape of leadership. *Educational Leadership*, 59(8), 61–63.

Krueger, C., Snow-Renner, R., and Ziebarth, T. (2002). State interventions in low-performing schools and school districts. Denver, CO: Education Commission of the States. Retrieved on February 17, 2004 from www.ecs.org.

Lashway, L. (2002). Developing Instructional Leaders. Eric Clearinghouse on Educational Management. Retrieved on August 7, 2007 from www.vtaide.come/png/ERIC/Developing-Instructional-Leaders.htm.

Leithwood, K. and Riehl, C. (2003). *What do we already know about successful school leadership?* Prepared for the AERA Division A Task Force on Developing Research in Educational Leadership.

Mintrop, H., MacLellan, A., and Quintero, H. (2001). School improvement plans in school on probation: A comparative content analysis across three accountability systems. *Educational Administration Quarterly*, 37(2), 197–218.

National Association of Elementary School Principals (2001). *Leading learning communities: Standards for what principals should know and be able to do.* Alexandria, VA: National Association of Elementary School Principals.

National Commission on Excellence in Education (1983). *A nation at risk.* Washington, DC: US Government Printing Office.

Newman, F., King, M., and Rigdon, M. (1997). Accountability and school performance: Implications from restructuring schools. *Harvard Educational Review*, 67(1), 41–47.

No Child Left Behind Act (2001). P.L. 107–110, sec. 1116 (b) (3).

O'Day, J., Goertz, M. E., and Floden, R. E. (1995). *Building Capacity for Educational Reform.* Philadelphia, PA: Consortium for Policy Research in Education.

Quinn, D. (2002). The impact of principal leadership behaviors on instructional practice and student engagement. *Journal of Educational Administration*, 40(4), 447–467.

Race to the Top (2009). *The White House: K-12 Education.* Retrieved on October 1, 2013 from www.whitehouse.gov/issues/education/k-12.

Seder, R. (2000). Balancing accountability and local control: State intervention for financial and academic stability. Policy Study No. 268.

Prepared for the Reason Public Policy Institute. Retrieved on February 17, 2004 from www.ecs.org.

Tyack, D. and Cuban, L. (1995). *Tinkering Toward Utopia.* Cambridge, MA: Harvard University Press.

United States Department of Education (2012). ESEA Flexibility. Retrieved on September 25, 2013 from www2.ed.gov/policy/elsec/guid/esea-flexibility/index.html.

Waters, T., Marzano, R., and McNulty, B. (2003). Balanced leadership: What 30 years of research tells us about the effect of leadership on student achievement. Retrieved on September 21, 2007 from www.mcrel.org/topics/Leadership/.

The Practice of Instructional Leadership

As a means of guiding your personal journey toward becoming an instructional leader you were asked in the previous chapter to reflect on what you currently believe an instructional leader does and why you currently believe you are or are not an instructional leader. You were also asked to identify a principal that you believe is an instructional leader and compare your practice to theirs. Did this cause more confusion or move you closer to clarity? Why is it that we have continued to be confused about what on the surface feels like it should be a fairly simple concept? A contributing factor may be the policies that are intended to improve the educational system themselves. In her study of small rural schools and NCLB implementation Lorna Jimerson (2005) pointed out that policies can become a barrier to their effective implementation. As I experienced in my own journey chasing policy requirements both created and reinforced the confusion of myself and my colleagues.

In the summer of 2014, I posted a survey on the National Association of Elementary School Principals' LinkedIn discussion group. The survey was intended to gain a better understanding of why we as a profession were struggling with developing both our understanding and practice of instructional leadership. The survey was completely voluntary, anonymous, and respondents self-selected into the sample. Representing twenty-nine states, the sixty-six respondents answered questions about whether or not they felt they were instructional leaders and whether or not policy influenced their practice. The majority of respondents felt they were instructional leaders but overwhelmingly that same group felt that policy changes had affected how they practiced instructional leadership. Longevity in a leadership role did not seem to influence that finding.

The Practice of Instructional Leadership

Table 2.1 LinkedIn Survey Results

		Less than 5 years	5–10 years	11–13 years	14 or more years	Total
If you are working as a school or district level administrator how long have you been in the role?						
Do you believe you are an instructional leader?	Yes	18	22	5	19	64
	No	0	1	0	1	2
Do you feel that changes in educational policy have affected how you practice instructional leadership?	Yes	12	17	2	18	49
	No	6	6	3	2	17
	Total	18	23	5	20	66

Drilling deeper into the idea that policy may influence practice, respondents were asked to share how they experienced that influence in their professional roles.

> Policy is usually heaped upon us from an outside source, local (District), state, or Federal. As a result, more of my time is consumed taking care of policy "stuff" and not being an instructional leader. At times I feel more like a manager.
> (Pk-5 Principal from NH with less than 5 years of experience)

> Since 1983 the role of the principal has changed from a school manager to an instructional leader. SB 813 required principals to be in the classroom 50% of their day. Hard to do with all of the disciplinary, budgetary, and administrative/Spec Ed meetings that occur each day.
> (Grade 6–8 Principal from CA with more than 14 years of experience)

There are only 24 hours in a day and management often takes most of that time.

(Pk-5 Principal from OH with less than 5 years of experience)

Today Instructional Leadership means I have to focus on the latest State mandates rather than helping teachers to improve their practice on a more personal level. I think we are losing the ability to help teachers develop the interpersonal component of teaching because we have to focus on data. I believe data is an effective tool, as well as standards but learning how to interact with students and teachers is just as important.

(Pk-5 Principal from TX with 5–10 years of experience)

Summarizing what was a common theme in survey responses, a high school principal from Nevada with less than five years of experience shared they did not feel they were an instructional leader and that they felt that way because "Our time is consumed with paperwork and mandates that make us more managers than instructional leaders." The results of the survey suggest that many principals feel that policy influences their ability to practice instructional leadership and they instead have been forced into the role of manager. In order to move forward on the journey to becoming an instructional leader we must then understand the difference between management and leadership and how to mitigate any negative influences of policy on our practice.

Management Versus Leadership

As pointed out by the survey principals, the current policy environment has created an unintended consequence of substituting the practice of management for instructional leadership for many school leaders. Adding to the confusion about what it means to be an instructional leader is the blurred line that has developed between the practice of management and the practice of leadership. This blurred line is often seen in job postings for principal positions in which the district is looking for a strong instructional leader that will ensure *compliance with mandates and regulations*. In order to begin to make sense of the instructional leadership paradigm, we must first be clear on the difference between management and leadership and why awareness of the difference matters.

Jim Collins (2001) articulated a continuum of traits that he found demonstrated by individuals in professional roles that were considered to be leadership positions. The continuum extended from management to leadership. What is clear from his continuum is that there is also a continuum of the quality of the human dynamic that exists between those in positions of authority and those that report to them. Levels 1 and 2 of the Collins continuum clearly show the focus on the person in authority. They make *individual contributions, contribute to the team,* and *work well with others*. In essence they are a member of the group that ensures the work that needs to be done gets done. Level 1 and 2 leaders *check off the boxes* of tasks that need to be completed. Those at level 3, although still characterized by Collins as managers, begin to create systems of people and resources in order to meet organizational goals. While those at levels 4 and 5 demonstrate a more substantial interpersonal dynamic through their ability to engage others with the realization of the organization's vision. The level 4 and 5 leaders in the Collins (2001) study demonstrate an ability to focus the organization and its constituents around a common mission and vision, inspire members of the organization to meet high expectations for performance and personal growth, and are willing to do whatever is necessary to ensure the success of the organization and those within it. In short, level 4 and 5 leaders are highly and significantly engaged with and in the people of the organization. These leaders can be described as dealing with the human issues. That is they attend to the inter- and intra-personal dynamics of the organization. Unlike those at level 1 and 2, levels 4 and 5 leaders are deeply invested in the human dynamic of the organization.

The overarching theories of transformational leadership and transactional leadership can be used to provide greater clarity to the difference between leadership and management. For our purposes these umbrella theories will be used as a means to organize the prominent theories of leadership that exist in the literature; transformational leadership includes servant leadership (Greenleaf, 1977), charismatic leadership (House, 1977), and the specific practice of transformational leadership (Bass, 1985), while transactional leadership includes the theories of contingent reward (Bass, 1990), management by exception (Bass, 1990), and laissez-faire (Bass, 1981). Common between the various theories is consideration for the human element in an organization and in particular how the individual in a leadership role perceives the needs of their constituents, interacts with those needs, and ultimately responds to the needs. In both the transformational and transactional oriented theories satisfying the organizational mission and making the vision a reality are the goals but how the human element of the process is supported, nurtured, and engaged as participants in that process are differentiators. In short, what these theories have in common is they address the interpersonal element of the organization that exists between those identified as the leader and those they are responsible for leading. Examination of transformational and transactional leadership and the leadership traits identified by Collins (2001) suggests that transactional type theories would encompass levels 1–3 while transformational types of theories would encompass levels 4 and 5.

Operationalized by Collins (2001) as leadership traits 1–3, the theories in the transactional leadership construct include: contingent reward, management by exception, and laissez-faire. In all three theories the leadership behaviors are less about the welfare of the individuals within the organization and more about the person identified as the boss accomplishing the organization's mission. In the field of education, the policies related to the high-stakes accountability movement of the last twenty years were predicated on the ideas of contingent-reward theory, using sanctions as a lever for improving student achievement (DiMaggio, 2003; Duffy, 2001; Krueger, Snow-Renner, & Ziebarth, 2002; No Child Left Behind, 2001; RttT, 2009). These policies, pushed down through the hierarchical system of public schooling, established goals for educators and consequences for not meeting them.

As was the case in my own professional experience many educators during that time experienced educational reforms as being based on a carrot-and-stick philosophy of management. Educators and entire schools were identified as underperforming and were punished by way of sanctions that included loss of funding, loss of employment, and school closures. As a solution to the new national problem of having a growing number of underperforming schools, state departments of education and school district administrators turned to quick-fix solutions that could be easily managed and supervised. Often forced by means of directives to oversee the

The Practice of Instructional Leadership

implementation of prescribed and scripted curriculum, rigid instructional delivery models, and other short-sighted quick fixes, the role of school principal began its transition from leader to manager.

Avolio, Waldman, and Yammarino in 1991 described leaders as needing to be ". . . more than merely a manager" (p. 9) and expanded that idea to include the four specific elements that comprise transformational leadership. Specifically, they identified transformational leaders as displaying

> ### *Box 2.1 Voices from Leaders in the Field*
>
> *Reading Specialist about Lisa:*
>
> I remember the meeting in the teacher's room. I'll never forget it. Lisa said, "We've been on this journey to figure out what the reading will look like in this school and after much research we've decided it's going to be the Literacy Collaborative Model and these people will be trained to be trainers. This is what will be happening for this school and how reading will be taught. If this isn't something you feel like you can support or be successful doing I can help you find another place to teach. I'd rather help you be teaching in a place you feel you can grow as a person and professional then for you to stay some place you don't." I had a lot of respect for her for saying it. Kind of like, this is the vision. This is where the majority of us see a clear, positive effect can happen for these kids. If you're not willing to go on this journey for these children then pretty much you don't belong here, and I'll help you find someplace else to teach but it also sent a clear message to us all that no matter who we were and what we believed she was genuinely committed to us as teachers and individuals developing and growing. I mean before we ever got here we spent months as a faculty engaged in research about literacy instruction. We asked questions and found the resources to answer them. She could have just told us what to do but she let us develop our expertise instead. Only one person asked to leave. She's teaching at another school in the district and is very happy. Lisa helped her find the right place for her to be successful and now she's a literacy leader in that school.

four distinct characteristics: "individualized consideration, intellectual stimulation, inspirational, motivational, and idealized influence" (p. 13). Through each of these traits leaders serve to develop the individuals within the organization so that they can both see problems as opportunities and pursue new ways of thinking about and addressing problems. They don't intimidate or punish to engage their subordinates but instead aide them in developing an ethical or moral purpose for taking action. Transformational leaders work from the perspective of growing the people in the organization so that the organization itself can flourish and achieve its mission.

In a 2013 meta-analysis Jackson, Meyer, and Wang examined the relationship between leadership, employee commitment to the organization, and culture. In their study they found a very strong correlation between transformational leadership behaviors and the commitment of employees to the organization. Utilizing Meyer and Allen's (1991) three themes of commitment they found a strong positive correlation between transformational leadership and affective commitment or the emotional attachment

Box 2.2 Voices from Leaders in the Field

Bob:

I really try to know where people's interests are so I can support them. When people are involved in the things they're passionate about they're happier at work and more likely to stay with us a while. So when educators come to work here, no matter what their role or how long they've been in the field, I really try to find that out about them. Who are they as individuals and professionals? What are their goals? What do they really get excited about doing? What are their strengths? I then can guide them to the places in the school where they can be most beneficial but that can also provide them the most satisfaction for their work and efforts. We've really developed our internal capacity that way to provide professional development opportunities but we've also ended up developing our teachers as leaders in the school and in the district. Most of them also end up pursuing graduate degrees because they want to learn more and be able to bring more back to try.

of employees ($p = .445$, p. 91) to the organization. While transactional leadership showed a much lower correlation[1], they also found a positive correlation between transformational leadership and normative commitment or sense of moral responsibility on the part of employees for the organization ($p = .337$, p. 92). As was the case with affective commitment the relationship between normative commitment and transactional leadership theories was much less[2]. The findings of this meta-analysis underscore the need to engage in transformational leadership behaviors in order to establish positive levels of commitment to the organization.

A second objective of the Jackson, Meyer, and Wang (2013) meta-analysis was to understand the influence of culture on the relationship between leadership and employee commitment. Although they defined culture through a national perspective it is not difficult to imagine their findings in the context of organizational culture. In particular they examined the influence of *individual-collectivism* or the difference between taking

---

Box 2.3 Voices from Leader in the Field

Helen:

I never do anything alone. I have decided that if I am going down, I am taking everyone with me [said jokingly]. So I never make a decision independently. That is number one. I am bringing everyone with me so let's jump together. I am very close to my assistant principal, who is in their second year, and my school counselor. I work very closely with teams of teachers. There is always a team decision.

Second Grade Teacher about Lisa:

She's all about the kids in this school. She runs morning math and whole school morning meeting. At lunchtime, takes them [students] all on a walk. If you work in this building, and you have a principal like that who's willing to go beyond and do things, I think that makes for a good foundation for change because you think, yeh, everybody's doing something.

care of yourself and your family versus being part of a social network in which you both feel responsible for the success of the group and believe that you'll be subsequently taken care of by it. As we consider organizational leadership, the idea of *individual-collectivism* is the difference between everyone in the organization working toward their own mission and the members of the organization working in collaboration to realize organizational goals.

While the findings of the Jackson, Meyer, and Wang (2013) meta-analysis did not suggest that individual-collectivism as a cultural dimension influenced the relationship between leadership and the affective and normative commitment of employees, it did not examine the question of whether leadership and employee commitment influence the level of

Box 2.4 Voices from Leaders in the Field

Bonnie:

I entered into a new building this year. They were terrorized the last couple of years. The last principal micromanaged everything they did. They couldn't make copies or fill out any forms. Everything needed her approval. My first goal was to get to know the faculty and where they're currently coming from in terms of the school and their needs. I sat down and had a 15-minute face-to-face meeting with every employee in the building. There are tons, it is a giant school and there are like seventy-seven people. I just asked them simple questions, like what do you love about this school? What would you change if you could? What do you need from me? Those kinds of questions. They all were so appreciative that I took the time to talk to them. The stuff they shared with me made it clear what they needed was to heal. So that's what we're working on the rest of this year and supporting them in developing their confidence and sense of value as people and professionals. Once we have that foundation we can build. It think it's easy to get caught up in getting things done but if you don't take the time to build relationships with your faculty what are you really going to accomplish?

individualism and collectivism in the organization. Findings from a study by Shaubroeck, Lam, and Peng (2011) would suggest that the answer to that question is that it does. Examining the development of employee trust for leaders, the researchers found that leaders that practiced transformational leadership developed trust-based relationships that resulted in increased team effectiveness. That is to say, when transformational leadership was practiced the members of the organization more effectively worked together to achieve goals; or from Jackson, Meyer, and Wang's (2013) perspective to enter into a state of collectivism.

As you can begin to see, understanding the difference between management and leadership is particularly important as we continue to consider our practice as instructional leaders and how we as leaders engage with our constituent groups for the purpose of realizing the school's vision and mission. Are we focused on developing the human element of our schools or are we just *checking the boxes* to ensure everything is getting done? Are we creating cultures that minimize individualism and support the development of collectivism or are we engaging in a process that points out and punishes the professional shortcomings of individuals without providing the appropriate support for improvement? Perhaps most importantly, how much time do we dedicate to developing authentic relationships with faculty and other community members?

The Practice of Instructional Leadership: An Introduction

Frequently defined in the literature by the school leader's focus on instruction, the pursuit of many principals to become instructional leaders has often been frustrating, confusing, and disheartening. Principals engage in the activities that researchers and subsequently policy-makers tell them they should engage in to both be an instructional leader and improve student achievement. Sadly, many don't experience the intended effects of instructional leadership in their school. As I and my colleagues had done, principals are continuing to ask, *what is instructional leadership*? As I reflect on my own journey perhaps a better question is, *what makes one principal's practice of instructional leadership more effective than another's*? The key to answering that question is in the name of the construct itself.

■ Instructional

The construct of instructional leadership is comprised of two words—instructional *and* leadership. Policy, researchers, and professional organizations have consistently defined instructional leadership through the elements of instructional practice—*the to-do list*. What has been inconsistent is how they define instructional leadership as a complete theory of practice. Principals on the LinkedIn survey were asked if they felt that the changing educational policies impacted their practice as instructional leaders. Sixty percent of those responding shared that they felt they did, expressing frustration with the demands placed on them by policies.

> With the advent of NCLB and the Common Core, principals are now required to not only manage programs and personnel, but also be Instructional Leaders as well. The problem is we really haven't been told how to do that. I wasn't trained to be an instructional leader as it's expected to be done today.
> (High School Principal from Illinois with over 14 years of experience)

> Really it's become about compliance and making sure the teachers are doing what the district says they're supposed to. My district requires me to complete a form every week that documents the objectives and standards have been posted in every classroom, lesson plans include everything the district requires, teachers are using the mandated materials and following the curriculum as it has been mapped, and that I have done a walkthrough evaluation lasting at least 30 minutes with follow up for 25 percent of my faculty. I have twenty teachers and 500 students—that doesn't leave much time for anything else. How can I possibly really practice leadership? I feel like I'm just holding the lid on.
> (Grades 5–8 Principal from New Mexico with 5–10 years of experience)

Changes in standards and assessments have mandated instructional changes. That's not a bad thing but the problem

> is we aren't given time to learn the new standards deeply, to align curriculum effectively, or to develop necessary instructional practices before new assessments are put into place. It's hard to provide instructional leadership when it feels like we're building the plane and learning to fly it at the same time.
>
> (Grades pk-5 Principal from Connecticut with over 14 years of experience)

What was clear from responding principals was that they felt that policy had a great deal of influence on their professional practice but they weren't always clear about what or how to meet the related demands.

In looking across the definitions of instructional leadership provided through policy, research, and professional organizations the focus on instructional practice can be seen as focused by four overarching themes. Specifically, instructional leadership has referred to a focus on learning for students and teachers, the communication of high expectations for student achievement and professional practice, engagement in data-based decision making, and the development of communities that are focused by a singular vision and mission for the school (Carrier, 2011; National Title I, 2015; NAESP, 2001; NCLB, 2001; NISL, 2004; Waters, Marzano, and McNulty, 2003). For the sake of our discussion and your journey to explore your instructional leadership practice we'll refer to those themes as defining the *work* of instructional leaders or the types of tangible activities they engage with over the course of time. While we'll go into each of the themes more fully in the next chapter a brief overview is provided here.

Focused on Learning

Learning is the primary focus of instructional leaders. While you may have just said, *ok I do that*, when you reflect on your focus on learning who is it that you are focused on? The focus for instructional leaders is not just on student learning but it's also on adult learning; including their own. While they focus on both children and adults, what's significant in how they focus on the learning of students is their focus on the whole child. While academics are important and they know their school will be publically judged through test scores, instructional leaders also recognize the

Box 2.5 Voices from Leaders in the Field

Doug:

It's about building on their [teachers] questions, their curiosity, and their strengths. If you're going to develop your faculty you have to start by understanding what they're curious about. For us it was technology. That was the interest of the teachers and the parents and school board too coincidentally. And I had an interest in technology so it was a great place for us to start. Before I got into education I worked in technology and so I kind of knew it from a business perspective, a marketing perspective. I could you know have a different lens as to what we wanted our students to be able to know, exposed to, to learn from; and, so that was kind of a commonality for us to work toward. It was new for them. It was new for me to think about technology in the educational spectrum and so we could learn together and we were building our trust and our practice.

---

importance of other types of learning that children need to engage in to be successful beyond the schoolhouse doors.

The result of the instructional leader's focus on learning is a highly engaged community of learners in which everyone is focused on learning; their own and the learning of others. The school communities that are led by instructional leaders can be appropriately defined as true professional learning communities (Dufour, Dufour, and Eaker, 2008). The sense of isolation that is experienced by many teachers dissolves in these schools and is replaced by a collaborative learning process. Instead of trying to solve the problems of student learning on their own, everyone becomes focused on developing the professional practice and educational programs of the school.

High Expectations

If you ask enough educators you'll begin to believe everyone has high expectations. Having high expectations has in many ways become part of

The Practice of Instructional Leadership

> ### Box 2.6 Voices from Leaders in the Field
>
> Bob:
>
> When teachers are new to our school I make a conscious effort to communicate to them about our expectations here for them. They are high. For example, it's expected that every educator will be actively engaged in developing their practice so that they can better meet the needs of the students. We don't even know today what they'll need tomorrow, so it's really important that educators do that. I make it clear that means they're a contributing member of our PLC; they're seeking out and participating in relevant professional development opportunities. It's not enough to go to a workshop they need to be clear about why they're going and how they'll implement and share what they learn. I remind them of that any time we meet to discuss their practice formally but also any other chance I can get to make sure that they remain conscious of the expectations and what they need to do to meet them.

the educational jargon. What does it mean to have high expectations? Who do we have high expectations for? How do we support others in understanding what we mean when we say we have high expectations? Instructional leaders clearly and consistently communicate to students, faculty, staff, parents, and the community that they have high expectations for student learning and professional practices. They not only say they have high expectations but they operationalize the term so everyone understands what meeting expectations looks and sounds like in practice. Additionally, instructional leaders model what they expect and hold themselves to the same expectations as they have for others.

Data-Based Decision Making

Educational reform policies of the early 21st century can be characterized as being predicated on data; specifically, the use of high-stakes testing data for determining school effectiveness. The increasing demand on educators to use data to make decisions about programming and instructional practices has been narrowly focused on the results of high-stakes testing andthe resulting policy prescribed levels of school performance (NCLB, 2001; US Department of Education, 2009). Although the recently signed Every Student Succeeds Act (2015) provides some hope for how data is used in accountability it remains to be seen how this hope will be realized in practice. Setting aside the myopically focused data use suggested by policy instructional leaders ensures that a variety of data sources are used to guide the decision making of schools. In addition to the data that is yielded from high-stakes testing and other formal tests of student achievement, instructional leaders ensure that a variety of qualitative and quantitative data sources are utilized in order to develop a holistic view of the school, its strengths, areas in need of growth, student achievement, and educational practices.

Box 2.7 Voices from Leaders in the Field

Lisa:

Yes the *tests* are important [ref. state test] but they aren't the be all and end all. We collect all kinds of data and make sure we look at each kid from all different angles. We collect reading, math, behavior, attendance, personal, and social. We have formative and summative assessments. Once a month a full day is scheduled for data team meeting. The reading specialist runs it for me. She brings in a special educator and title 1 teacher and every grade level meets with them to go over every kid. Are they going up on something? Are they going down? What does the data tell us may be causing that? If they're going down they figure out together based on the data how to turn that around. If they went up they work out what's working and how that can be built on. Yes they're going to get the state test but that's not going to provide them nearly the level of information they need to move kids along and they don't help with getting the whole picture on kids.

■ Developing Communities Around a Single Vision and Mission

Often misunderstood and underused, vision and mission statements provide a framework for schools to gauge their decision making, practices, and outcomes against. For the purpose of developing our common understanding in this book, vision will be defined as a dream for a future reality, and mission will be defined as the actions that will be taken to realize that future. Martin Luther King's (1963) *I Have a Dream* speech is arguably the best example of clear articulation of a leader's vision and mission. Throughout the speech Dr. King signalled us to his *vision* or dream for the future and then immediately told us what he felt needed to happen to make that dream reality. For those more comfortable with a sports analogy consider an NFL football coach. They have a vision or dream each year to win the Super Bowl. Their mission is to win each game along the way. In service to realizing their vision they lead their teams in a manner they feel will inspire them to work hard on developing the skills and play needed to win enough games during the season to make it to the playoffs and then ultimately to win the championship. In order to keep their teams positively engaged in each mission, or regular season game, coaches seek opportunities throughout the season to engage team members in the vision. In both examples the leader (Dr. King and the football coach) uses vision and mission to catalyze their communities. The vision acts as a unifying force that supports members of the organization in developing and acting on their commitment to the community and each other.

All schools are supposed to in theory have a vision and mission. Many schools have beautifully crafted vision and/or mission statements. Some schools do not have an agreed on vision and/or mission. In other cases the presence of vision and mission statements are obvious and in others they are not. It has become more and more common for schools to post vison and mission statements in visible locations like school entry ways and classroom walls. But what purpose do they provide in the school? How are they being used to catalyze the school into a unified community? In the case of instructional leaders the use of vision and mission is deliberate. They not only make sure that they are visible; they make sure they are easily understood by everyone in the community and that everyone understands them. Instructional leaders model the vision and mission—

> ### Box 2.8 Voices from Leaders in the Field
>
> *Bonnie:*
>
> Now that I'm in a new building I'm spending time learning about it. I've been spending a lot of time in classrooms in the last few weeks, trying to get a handle on what's happening there. The first few weeks, though, I spent having individual face-to-face meetings with each of the faculty and staff. I really wanted to understand what they like about school, what they would change, what they want the school to be like, and what they need from me. Now I have a better sense of their vision and the gap between that and where we are now. Now we can use that to develop our vision for the school together. It's not about me and my personal vision but about us and our vision together that we're going to work toward making reality.

in other words they don't just *talk the talk* they are purposeful and deliberate about *walking the walk*.

No One Way

Through my research with the exemplar principals what has become clear is that there is not one way that instructional leaders engage in their *work*. How the principal demonstrates a focus on each of the components is influenced by personal strengths, a particular point in time of their career or school's history, and school context. The variance in how instructional leaders engage in their *work* is best described as having either a direct or indirect influence on student achievement: the principal doing something themselves to affect student achievement or the principal enabling others in the organization to take action in in order to affect student achievement. Whether a principal applies direct or indirect influence does not exalt or diminish them as instructional leaders. It simply indicates they are attending in some way to the issue of instruction in their school.

Many of you are reading this section and saying, *but I do all that why isn't it working?* The answer lies in the second word of the instructional leadership construct—*leadership*.

Leadership

As we've explored earlier there is a difference between the practice of management and the practice of leadership. Managers attend to the *checklist of tasks* while leaders also attend to the human dynamic. While there's been a clear focus on the instructional side of the practice of instructional leadership, have we lost sight of the leadership side of the construct? I offer to you that in fact we have. One need only look to recent federal educational legislation to evidence the lack of attention to this element (National Title I, 2015; USDOE, 2012). Absent from both the ESEA Flexibility Waivers of 2012 (USDOE, 2012) and Every Student Succeeds Act of 2015 is the mention of leadership behaviors. With regard to the practice of school leadership the focus is singularly defined through the instructional component of instructional leadership or the *work* of principals. Through these pieces of legislation the articulated focus of school leaders is instructional practice, student assessment data, and the assessment of student achievement as a tool for measuring the professional practice of educators (Carrier, 2014). What these pieces of legislation have missed is the practice of *leadership*. Could it be that the assumption is that leadership will just happen? That it's somehow innate to those that rise to positions of authority in schools and doesn't require a deliberate focus? Or is there a lack of a working operational definition of leadership that can be used as a touchstone for the development of legislation and policy? The answers to those questions are not clear but what is clear is assessing the construct of leadership is a challenge that policy-makers haven't taken up.

Research on instructional leadership has further served to segment the instructional leadership construct. Most notable are the emerging studies that compare instructional leadership to other theories of leadership practice. Studies on instructional leadership are most often focused by the element of instruction. (Shatzer, Caldarella, Hallam, & Bron, 2014). In their comparison of what they identified as two different theories of leadership practice—instructional leadership and transformational leadership—Shatzer et al. (2014) found that instructional leadership as they defined it has a slightly greater effect on student achievement than transformational leadership. What I've observed in my research is that the technical skills identified through the element of instruction were not enough to move schools forward. While the principals studied either directly or indirectly engage in each of the elements of the *work* deemed necessary for instructional leaders, it was their *leadership* behaviors that made the difference. In short, a holistic practice of instructional leadership that includes both the instruction and leadership elements is required in order to have an effective practice.

Questions for Reflection and Discussion

1. As you reflect on the *work* of instructional leaders how are each of the themes evidenced in your practice?
2. Think back to the principal you identified in Chapter 1's *Questions for Reflections and Discussion*. How is each of the themes we've identified as the *work* of principals demonstrated in their practice?
3. How is leadership and management demonstrated in your current practice? Which appears more strongly in your practice?
4. As you continue to think about the principal you identified in Chapter 1's *Questions for Reflections and Discussion*, how are management and leadership demonstrated in their practice?
5 To what extent do you feel you engage in a holistic practice of instructional leadership? In what ways do you engage in *both* the work and the leadership components of the construct?

Notes

1 Contingent reward $p = .369$, Management by exception $p = -.083$, and Laissez-faire $p = -.296$ (p. 91).
2 Contingent reward $p=.281$, Management by exception $p = .111$, and Laissez-faire $p = -.164$ (p. 92).

References

Avolio, B., Waldman, D., and Yammarino, F. (1991). Leading in the 1990s: The four I's of transformational leadership. *The European Journal of Industrial Training*, 15(4), 9–16.

Bass, B. M. (1981). *Stogdill's Handbook of Leadership: A survey of theory and research.* New York: Free Press.

Bass, B. M. (1985). *Leadership and Performance Beyond Expectations.* New York: Free Press.

Bass, B. M. (1990). From transactional to transformational leadership: Learning to share the vision. *Organizational Dynamics,* 18(3), 19–31.

Carrier, L. (2011). *What is instructional leadership and what does it look like in practice? A multi-case case study of elementary school principals who have led schools from being identified as underperforming to performing.* University of Massachusetts, MA: Doctoral dissertation.

Carrier, L. (2014). If we want to really improve our schools we need to make leadership a priority for instructional leaders. *The New Hampshire Journal of Education,* 17, 58–63.

Collins, J. (2001) *Good to Great.* New York: Harper Collins.

DiMaggio, M. (2003). State support to low-performing schools. Washington, DC: The Chief State School Officers. Retrieved on February 18, 2004 from www.ecs.org.

Duffy, M. (2001). *America's reform inferno: The nine layers of accountability.* Paper presented at the annual meeting of the American Educational Research Association. Seattle, WA.

Dufour, R., Dufour, R., and Eaker, R. (2008). *Revisiting professional learning communities.* Bloomington, IN: Solution Tree.

Greenleaf, R. (1977). *Servant Leadership: A journey into the nature of legitimate power and greatness.* New York: Paulist Press.

House, R. J. (1977). A 1976 theory of charismatic leadership. In J. G. Hunt and L. L. Larson (Eds.) Leadership: The cutting edge. Carbondale, IL: Southern Illinois University Press, pp. 189–207.

Jackson, T., Meyer, J., & Wang, X. (2013). Leadership, commitment, and culture. A meta-analysis. *Journal of Leadership and Organizational Studies,* 20(1), 84–106.

Jimerson, L. (2005). Placism in NCLB—How rural children are left behind. *Equity and Excellence in Education,* 38(30), 211–219.

King, M. L. (1963). I have a dream. Retrieved on January 9, 2016 from www.americanrhetoric.com/speeches/mlkihaveadream.htm.

Krueger, C., Snow-Renner, R., and Ziebarth, T. (2002). State interventions in low-performing schools and school districts. Denver, CO: Education Commission of the States. Retrieved on February 17, 2004 from www.ecs.org.

Meyer, J. and Allen, N. (1991). A three component conceptualization of organizational commitment. *Human Resource Management Review*, 1(1), 61–89.

National Association of Elementary School Principals (2001). *Leading learning communities: Standards for what principals should know and be able to do.* Alexandria, VA: National Association of Elementary School Principals.

National Institute of School Leadership (2004). *The Educational Challenge: Instructor's Guide. Course one.*

National Title I Association (2015). ESEA Reauthorization Bill Becomes Law. Retrieved on January 13, 2016 from www.titlei.org/news-and-resources/blogs/legislation/esea-reauthorization-bill- becomes-law.

No Child Left Behind Act (2001). P.L. 107–110, sec. 1116 (b) (3). (2001). Retrieved on January 13, 2016 from www.nochildleftbehind.com/nclb-law-contents.html.

Race to the Top (2009). *The White House: K-12 Education.* Retrieved on October 1, 2013 from www.whitehouse.gov/issues/education/k-12.

Shatzer, R., Caldarella, P., Hallam, R., and Bron, B. (2014). Comparing the effects of instructional leadership and transformational leadership on student achievement: implications for practice. *Educational Management Quarterly*, 42(4), 445–459.

Shaubroeck, J., Lam, S., and Peng, A. (2011). Cognition-based and affect-based trust as mediators of leader behavior influences on team performance. *The Journal of Applied Psychology*, 96(4), 863–871.

United States Department of Education (2009). The American recovery and reinvestment act of 2009: Saving and creating jobs and reforming education. US Department of Education. Retrieved on September 16, 2009 from www2.ed.gov/policy/gen/leg/recovery/implementation.html.

United States Department of Education (2012). ESEA Flexibility. Retrieved on October 20, 2012 from www2.ed.gov/policy/elsec/guid/esea-flexibility/index.html.

Waters, T., Marzano, R., and McNulty, B. (2003). Balanced leadership: What 30 years of research tells us about the effect of leadership on student achievement. Retrieved on September 21, 2007 from www.mcrel.org/topics/Leadership.

3 | The Work of the Principal

In the previous chapters we've established a foundation, the groundwork from which our professional learning community can develop. We've acknowledged our confusion and lack of clarity about what instructional leadership is and is not, clarified the role of school principals in the 21st century and their moral imperative to become instructional leaders, compared leadership to management, and begun to define a framework for the practice of instructional leadership. As you've reflected on your practice I'm hopeful that your questions have begun to move away from those that are focused by *Am I or aren't I an instructional leader?* and more toward those focused by *How can I develop and refine my instructional leadership practice?* In this chapter we will move deeper into that exploration through closer consideration of one half of the instructional leadership model—*the work* of principals.

- focuses on learning for students and adults
- communicates high expectations for student achievement and instruction
- uses data to inform the work of the school
- develops a community that is unified around one vision and one mission for the school

Figure 3.1 The Work of the Principal
Source: Carrier, 2011

Focuses on Learning

Throughout modern history there has been a common understanding of the purpose of the public school in the United States—to ensure an educated populace so that communities could thrive. In the earliest years of colonization in the United States that idea was grounded in the idea that schools served as tools for the socialization of youth (Cremin, 1970). Regardless of how that idea has evolved over time at the most simplistic level of understanding, we as educators are charged with ensuring that curriculum is delivered, and that students learn the concepts and skills that are in that curriculum so that they can meaningfully contribute to the success of communities. Thus we are charged as a professional field with being focused on learning. Hopefully the curriculum that is delivered is relevant to students and facilitates them in developing the level of thinking skills that will support them in life beyond the schoolhouse, but fundamentally at its most basic form we are all as educators charged with the delivery of curriculum and oversight of student learning so that we as a nation can thrive. Reports like *A Nation at Risk* (1983) and educational policies like No Child Left Behind (2001) and Race to the Top (2009) have served to focus our attention on the need for rigorous academic environments that would ultimately ensure our economic success as a nation in the global economy. The reforms of the 1990s and early 2000s brought the standards-based movement of educational reform into practice and focused our view of learning through the lens of student mastery of the identified sets of standards. Sadly, those same reforms brought the high-stakes accountability movement and requirement that students pass state testing at a prescribed level of performance with scores being used to rate schools—for the first time in our history student test scores were used to formally assess the effectiveness of schools and provided a mechanism for providing rewards and sanctions to schools and educators. Also for the first time in the modern history of the U.S. public education system, school principals were being formally held accountable for student achievement as it was being measured by high-stakes testing. The result was a new and often troubling perspective of how we as a profession focused on learning—test scores and their improvement as a singular indictor of learning.

While the reforms of the late 20th and early 21st centuries were meant to increase student achievement, the 2015 NAEP results suggest they did not have that intended effect. As a tool for considering the impact of national reforms, the 2015 reports demonstrated that achievement, as measured by average scaled scores, in reading at grade 4 had not increased significantly from 2002 (+4 points) and that the grade level had only grown by one point from 2013. Similarly grade 8 reading results showed non-significant growth between 2002 and 2013 (+1) and of more concern showed a decrease in performance of three points between 2013 and 2015. In mathematics, grade 4 also demonstrated low growth between 2003 and 2015 (+5) and grade 8 demonstrated the same low growth (+4). More troubling is that both grade levels demonstrated a decline in mathematics from the 2013 level of performance in math. The stated intention of high-stakes accountability is that all students reach proficiency on the prescribed

---

Box 3.1 Voices from Leaders in the Field

Doug:

As an instructional leader I would say it's really about creating the conditions for success; for teachers to deliver instruction and for students to receive instruction and become independent learners. So I'm not the instructor. I am not the teacher. I'm not in the class on a daily basis teaching. But what I can do is I can create the weather. I can create the environment. Does it feel warm and comfortable? Can risks be taken? Do teachers feel supported? Do we have the resources teachers need? It's really about creating the conditions for high quality instruction to occur, but I'm not going to bring the instruction.

Helen:

As instructional leaders we're charged with leading the learning that happens in our schools. That means my involvement in all areas of the curriculum is necessary. I roll my sleeves up and help teachers unpack and understand it. To develop common language and competencies and then from there ensuring curriculum, instruction, and assessment are all aligned vertically across the school and horizontally across grade levels and between us and the schools we are fed by and feed.

curriculum standards. The 2015 NAEP results demonstrate that the reforms are not meeting their intended goal. Clearly our myopic test-focused view of learning has not had the impact on student achievement that was intended.

Instructional leaders resist viewing learning strictly through the lens of high-stakes testing results. While instructional leaders acknowledge that

Box 3.2 *Voices from Leaders in the Field*

Penny:

For me the school is my classroom now only I'm responsible for the learning of many more individuals. Just like the children our teachers are our students. It's not about the summative evaluation. For the most part that's not going to do much to support learning for your teachers. It's the formative process that includes "instruction." What is the objective for them? What do you really want them to know and be able to do? How do you need to scaffold their learning to get them there? I really spend the time getting to know them as learners. How do they learn? What do they need to include new learning in their practice? Then I develop a curriculum and instructional plan so that everyone is set up to be successful and to grow.

Bob:

One of the things that became clear was that teachers needed time to work together as researchers of practice. That's how they engage in their professional and to some degree personal learning here. They work together as researchers that are examining their practice and researching new and potentially better ways of doing something and then studying its effect. It's important that they have that time for learning if we want them to be able to keep moving kids forward and if want them to be able to develop the types of classrooms kids need to best prepare them for their future. So we gutted the schedule and redesigned it to include that time and provided them with professional development for how to engage in that type of learning and support to get it going. I guess you can say they're my students too and I'm making sure they can achieve at high levels.

test scores are important they do not view them as a singular reflection of learning or educator effectiveness. Instead instructional leaders view learning as a broader more robust construct that applies to everyone in their school's community, including the adults. That is they consider everyone in their school community learners and take responsibility for ensuring each learner in their care achieves at the highest level possible.

While it has become a common criticism that educators teach to the test, instructional leaders look beyond test results to develop the delivered curriculum, ensuring that each learner's needs are met and that each can progress on a realistic but rigorous learning path. They consider what has become commonly known as the *whole child* and have applied that concept to all ages of learners in their schools. Instructional leaders are concerned with each individual in the organization and how to best ensure they can access learning opportunities so that each can achieve growth.

For instructional leaders learning is the core technology of schools. They encourage, support, and expect that everyone in the school regardless of their age or position is meaningfully engaged in learning. Students are expected to be actively engaged in their own learning and not to interfere with the learning of others. Educators are expected to be engaged in their own personal and professional learning, as well as the learning of the professional community. Additionally, educators are expected to be engaged in the learning of the parent community and the segment of the community that does not have children in the school.

Box 3.3 Voices from Leaders in the Field

Terry:

I try to be in classrooms for some part of every day. It may not be very long but for at least some part of the day. I'm not really there to be watching over the teachers, I really trust them to do their job. I want to remind the kids, especially the ones that might be struggling, that they're part of our team here and their job on the team is to focus on their learning and to make sure they don't disrupt their friends from doing their job. We're all here to learn.

Box 3.4 Voices from Leaders in the Field

Lisa:

I remember when my nephews were learning to read and I said Sally, [Lisa's sister] all you have to do is do this to help them. She said, Lisa, you understand how to do that. I don't understand how to do that. So I thought, yah, here's a college-educated person who doesn't understand how to do that reading thing; so it made me realize that lots of parents don't understand that so show them what they *can* do. We bring parents in one on one and run workshops for them too so we can show them how to help their kids.

Penny:

One of our challenges is that the community doesn't always understand what we do here or why we do it. It really comes up when it comes to getting the budget passed. We were hearing a lot of "it worked for me why do they need that" type of language. We realized we needed to educate the community, especially those that maybe didn't have kids in the schools. So we started finding opportunities to display student work all over town. It was in almost every store front on Main Street. Then we got a little more high tech and started posting QR codes around town that linked to student work, curriculum, volunteer opportunities, and other school information. We started getting questions about what types of learning activities were happening at the school so we started bringing student groups to different community venues to present their work and teachers did workshops for parents and community members on how to support struggling readers, support mathematical learning. We hear less of that non-supportive language at budget time and we've seen an increase in volunteers that don't have children of their own in the school.

Critical to this is that instructional leaders include themselves in that expectation and are purposeful in modeling for students, educators, and parents what it means to be focused on learning. Instructional leaders are themselves learners and model the value and importance of that in all they do. As an instructional leader, I feel strongly that it is my responsibility to model for my constituents the importance of being an active, engaged learner. In addition to my personal pursuit of formal education as a school principal, I engaged in professional development and training activities with my faculty and staff. If they were expected to be there, so was I. Together we'd analyze how what we were learning could benefit our kids and process how to integrate what we learned into the practices of our school. My professional reading list, as well as the books my personal children and I were reading together, was posted proudly on my office door. I actively sought out opportunities to engage students, parents, and teachers in what I was reading and encouraged them to share what they were reading with me. It wasn't just a matter of leaving an article in a mailbox but of engaging in the discourse of learning with colleagues about its contents. I openly shared what I was learning, always careful to cite where this new knowledge was coming from and my thinking about how and why it might be useful to our work together. While it was sometimes shocking to my students that I too was a student, for my teachers my explicit modeling of my own learning sparked the pursuit of their own curiosities and they too began to share their learning with others.

Communicates High Expectations

High expectations have sadly become part of the jargon in education and, like most buzz words, they have lost any sense of common understanding in our society. Educator evaluations include assessment of whether high expectations are communicated to students and whether they exist in practice. But what does it mean to have high expectations? Most often when we listen to educators talking about expectations they're referring to students meeting policy defined testing benchmarks that describe how close a student is to mastering a set of curriculum standards. If we accept that as our definition of expectations, and in particular high expectations, what then are our expectations for those students that have already mastered or exceeded mastery of the targeted curriculum standards? Reflecting on the 2015 NAEP results it's incumbent on us to ask, *has the common contemporary understanding of high expectations well-served students?* The data would suggest that it has not.

To begin to explore the idea of high expectations and how they connect to the practice of instructional leaders let's first examine the term itself. The Merriam Webster Learner's Dictionary (n.d.) defines *expectation* as:

- a belief that something will happen or is likely to happen;
- a feeling or belief about how successful, good, etc., someone or something will be.

And the word *high* as:

- rising or extending upward a great distance;
- extending or reaching upward more than other things of the same kind;
- located far above the ground or another surface.

In the context of being focused on learning, *high expectations* can be defined then as a belief that every learner will demonstrate growth on curriculum benchmarks and educational program outcomes at the uppermost level possible. In that same way that we are beginning to understand in our profession that fair isn't always equal (Wormelli, 2006), high expectations

Box 3.5 Voices from Leaders in the Field

Lisa:

It's simple. You're not going to disrupt the learning of other kids. That does not happen. You're not allowed to do that. If you do, then you're out [time out in another room or the office] not them. I tell students that and I have that conversation with parents. If it becomes an issue, they're out more than twice they get put on a behavior plan and the parents are required to sign it every day and have to meet with me before it's discontinued. Some don't like it but they all do it because they know our only concern here is the kids. We always go back to that. How is what we're doing right now in this moment going to serve your child in their future?

are not one size fits all. They are instead customized to the learner in order to support them in moving toward mastery of identified learning benchmarks regardless of their individual starting point.

Instructional leaders communicate that definition of high expectations every day through their verbal and written communications and their professional practice. They possess a clear operational definition of their expectations that is founded upon their mission to be focused on learning. Contrary to the educational policies that place test-determined levels of achievement as central, these leaders keep learning before achievement

Box 3.6 Voices from Leaders in the Field

Bonnie:

If you want them [ref. teachers] to "buy-in" to the expectations sometimes you really need work with them to help them to see them almost on their own. We'll start here in this school by beginning our conversation around what are you doing? Why are you doing it? and How do you know it's working? Then I'll lead some learning walks in classrooms that I feel are exemplars at this point. We'll then process our learning walks to articulate as a group what the expectations for instructional practice should be in the building. I could just deliver a mandate but if I really want them to feel safe enough to begin to challenge their own practice I need them to see where we're headed not just tell them. They need to see it's possible. Once the expectation is agreed on then I can provide the support they need to engage in their own growth process and ultimately hold them accountable if they don't get there.

Bob:

We have a pretty strong evaluation system. The rubrics are well developed and they really operationalize what's expected to be considered effective. Even though I don't hold evaluation over their heads, I really want that process to be about professional learning and growth; we do go back to that in order to stay focused and in agreement about what the expectations for practice are.

and consider assessments as a means to understanding the depth and breadth of learning. Instructional leaders have high expectations not just for the students in their schools but for the professional practice of the school's educators, and for the involvement of parents in the educational process. The expectations are not just words but their communication is a process of teaching what it looks and sounds like when expectations are being met. They embed their expectations into the culture of the school through the development of norms that ensure adherence to them. Instructional leaders have a great deal of clarity about their expectations and consistently and concisely communicate, model, and reinforce them in the school, so that they become the norm or *how we do it here*. As a result all members of the school community from the youngest student, to teachers, parents, and community members at large know exactly what is expected of learners in the school and what it looks like when members meet expectations.

Data-Based Decision Making

Schools have always been full of data. We've collected and stored enrollment, attendance, behavior, and academic data about our students. Teacher evaluations have been conducted and safely stored in filing cabinets, and personnel seniority lists have been carefully maintained. In this way we have traditionally been data rich. We have gathered lots of information about the members of our school communities; some for regulatory and statutory compliance, and some because it's what seems to have been always done. We may not always be clear about why, but we collect data and if we were asked for it we could provide the appropriate manila folder, binder, or other containment system full of the requested information.

The educational policies of the 1990s and early 2000s mandated the use of data for decision making. This was realized through the inclusion of particular data points (i.e. attendance, high school graduation rate, test scores) into state accountability formulas. In response, educators became richer with regard to the data we amassed, but in most cases we become impoverished in terms of the information we had about our schools—we became more *data rich* but we also very often became *more information poor*. While the policies mandated the use of data they did not provide support for developing the instructional and leadership capacities of schools to effectively use data for decision making (NCLB, 2001; US Department of Education, 2009). Combined with the carrot-and-stick mind set of the educational policies themselves, the lack of support for capacity building often resulted in educators being overwhelmed by the volume of data, and with data often not being effectively utilized to inform the educational processes of schools.

Beyond the overarching impact of developing a professional culture of inquiry, studies have found that the establishment of data-based decision making (DBDM) as a school-wide process further impacts the organization through its effects on teachers and students. Through the heightened awareness and understanding of data and inquiry, educators become more reflective about their practice and less accepting of initial answers (Carrier & Whaland, 2015; Feldman & Tung, 2001; Noyce, Perda, & Traver, 2000; Robinson, Bursuck, & Sinclair, 2013). Simply, it's no longer considered adequate or sufficient in schools to accept the surface level explanation of

Box 3.7 *Voices from Leaders in the Field*

Author:

In my own practice as an instructional leader the use of data for decision making was central. My concern became that data was becoming *my* issue and not *our* tool for making decisions about instruction, programs, and the school broadly. One of the reasons that seemed to be happening was access and a process for how to use the data. In order to make sure that everyone had access, they knew what do with it, and that there was a space that could maintain confidentiality a data room was developed. The room, close by the main office, held binders full of the variety of data we collected. A conference table, adequate seating, and the necessary supplies were maintained. Most importantly we scheduled time during the day for teams to meet there so that I could support them in learning a process of data inquiry. Based on the work of Nancy Love (2004) and Victoria Bernhardt (2003) the process both supported teachers in engaging with the data and supported them in transforming into an authentic and highly functioning professional learning community.

data. Educators in schools that have established DBDM processes readily ask the deeper questions that lead to rich and robust discourse about practice and educational programs. As a result of being better informed about programs and practices as a professional community they can then more strategically establish priorities (Carrier & Whaland, 2015; Noyce et al., 2000) and more articulately communicate those priorities with parents and the community.

"Data-driven school cultures do not arise in a vacuum" (Noyce et al., 2000, p. 54). Instructional leaders know this and are deliberate in the development of the use of data in their schools. They don't accept a single data point as absolute evidence; instead of using data as either a carrot or stick, they use it to inform and support learners in their work of meeting the high expectations that they have established. In service to that, instructional leaders ensure that a variety of data points are used to make decisions. In essence they work as a researcher might. First, instructional leaders clearly define the questions of student achievement and professional practice to be answered, then by gathering multiple data points they seek to ensure the trustworthiness of their findings.

Box 3.8 Voices from Leaders in the Field

Helen:

We focus a lot on data here. That is important, whether it's quantitative or qualitative, whether we are looking at numbers, students and teacher perceptions, it is all equally important. That drives decision making.

There is a multitude of ways to collect data. We collect formative and summative assessment data as well as survey data. We use surveys with parents, with our fifth graders when they leave the school for the middle school, and with teachers. We take all of that together and look across it all to identify our areas of strength and areas we need to develop. We never accept one data point as evidence of anything. It just generates a question that we then go looking someplace else to find more about or to start to develop a potential answer.

Facilitates a Unified Vision and Mission

It is likely that as a school leader your school has an existing vision and mission statement. If your school does have one or both of these guiding statements the degree to which they're known or used may vary. Likewise school vision and mission statements are as varied as their use. Often complex examples of lofty prose, these statements are rarely known and understood by constituents and subsequently don't find their way into the professional practices of the school. As my graduate students frequently tell me, "My principal says they think we have one but doesn't know where it is" or "We have one but I've never seen it and we never talk about it." The lack of consciousness of vision and mission leaves the school as an organization without a strong guidepost for decision making or means of assessing alignment of practice with accepted values. It also leaves it without a point of unification of purpose for the members of the school community.

There are strong examples of effectively used vision and mission statements that can be found in our cultural history. Effectively used vision

---

Martin Luther King Jr.'s I Have a Dream Speech (1963)

Vision Statement: I have a dream that my four children will one day live in a nation where they will not be judged by the color of their skin but by the content of their character.

Mission Statement: We must forever conduct our struggle on the high plane of discipline and dignity.

Ronald Reagan, First Inaugural Address (1981)

Vision Statement: Government has no power except that granted it by the people.

Mission Statement: It is my intention to curb the size and influence of the Federal establishment and to demand recognition of the distinction between the powers granted to the Federal Government and those reserved to the states or to the people.

Figure 3.2 Samples of Vision and Mission from Cultural History

and mission statements serve as a catalyst for organizations and ensure that everyone is working toward the same goal. Effective vision and missions are carefully crafted, clearly articulated by leaders, and explicitly connected to each other. They are also modeled in the day-to-day life of the leader. As a result, constituents can not only repeat the vision and mission, they know why each exists, and can identify with their underlying values. In this way constituents become unified around the vision and mission and work collectively to make the vision a reality and to successfully achieve the supporting mission(s).

Box 3.9 Voices from Leaders in the Field

Bob:

We worked as a school community to develop our vision and mission. They're based on our shared values and we use them to measure our decisions against. There are some things as educators we just have to do and how we get there is a conversation. When new policies and regulations come from the feds or state we don't just implement things here. We take the time to unpack them and see how they fit with what we're doing. If things are going to help us with realizing our vision and mission we make that connection and implement that piece completely. If it doesn't benefit our vision and mission we don't do it or we do what we need to in order to be in compliance. We don't throw everything out because of something new coming at us from outside.

Back in the NCLB days kids had to demonstrate their learning on high-stakes state tests. We knew they had to take the test but we didn't spend our time on kill and drill teaching, test taking strategies, or adding lots of other formal assessments to see if they were going to pass the state test. Instead, we focused on developing our instructional practice and deeply understanding the standards and how to facilitate learning so the students could master them. Not because of the state test but because we wanted to make sure they were prepared for success, whether they were going to college, the military, or a job, when they graduated. That's our vision for our kids.

Much like the leaders shared in Figure 3.2, instructional leaders ensure that the vision and mission of their school are well known, understandable, and that they model the vision and mission for everyone in the organization through their own behavior. They consistently use the vision and mission as a means of determining the alignment of practices to accepted values and as guideposts for the prioritization of resources and the work to be done. The cultural norms infused into the school through the work of the principal are strongly connected to the vision and its supporting mission(s). Additionally, vision and mission become a catalyst for the school constituents to rally around. They provide a sense of purpose for initiatives and programs and sense of identity to the school's community.

Like many school leaders you might have inherited a vision and mission that have ended in their utility. Often new principals tell me they are "stuck" with an old vision and mission. As a result of not feeling they can stand behind the vision the school as an organization lacks focus and actions become disjointed—in essence *everyone is paddling the*

Box 3.10 Voices from Leaders in the Field

Bonnie:

We did a whole number of things, all of the little kids' school photos, we put them up on a board in the school library, percentage of kids that were at goal, which at the time was about 35% of the kids—350 kids at the time. We put 35% of their little faces on one side and 65% that weren't functioning at grade level on the other. Then we asked is this ok? Does this work for us that 2/3 of our school is functioning below grade level? Look at their faces, does this work for us? Everyone wanted it to be better.

It was powerful because of their faces. It wasn't about the state test it was about the kids as whole students and how they were doing in relation to grade level and they weren't just numbers or reports they had faces. Faces we know and that belong to kids we love. It didn't take much convincing after that to get folks on board with developing their professional practice and with doing that together as a community.

The Work of the Principal

boat in a different direction. Instructional leaders don't accept the outdated or status quo. They work collaboratively with the school community to define and create a new vision that will serve as a north star for the work to be done.

As the instructional leader of an urban middle school that had been declared underperforming under a previous principal, I was faced with exactly that issue. The school had a vision and mission and the majority of the faculty viewed them as obsolete, while a few of the veterans believed that as long as they were in place they needed to compliantly adhere to them. The result was a school divided with one group going in one direction and the other going in all the variety of directions they felt were necessary to do their jobs. The divide often caused disagreement between faculty members. The inconsistency contributed to behavioral issues among students, loss of learning time, and the low test scores that ultimately triggered the designation of underperforming. The lack of agreed vision and mission left parents, school board members, and the community at large with no clear idea of what we as a school believed or valued.

Box 3.11 Voices from Leaders in the Field

Author:

Developing our vision and mission as a school was really about understanding our individual missions and the vision each of us had for our kids. During our opening of the school year faculty meeting I handed out markers and chart paper and assigned faculty and staff to groups. The groups were grade level specific. I then posed the question. We're starting a new school year, who are the kids that will be coming to us? Everyone looked a looked a little confused and one of the more vocal teachers asked, "Do you mean what are their names?" "No", I said, "Who are they as individuals? What will they look like, sound like, behave like? What are their likes and dislikes and interests? Who are these people that we'll be welcoming into our school?" I asked them to use the chart paper and markers to share their vision of who the kids coming to us the next day were; however they would like to do that. The groups each engaged in rich conversations about their vision for the kids at the beginning of the school year. Together they drew pictures, wrote poems and songs, and created lists of characteristics that shared their vision with the rest of the faculty and staff. Words like scared, disorganized, lost, socially uncomfortable, and academically struggling permeated the conversation. After they had all shared their work I then asked them to reflect on who they hoped the kids would be on the last day of school. They again drew pictures, wrote poems and songs, and made lists but this time words like confident, resilient, responsible, respectful, socially connected, and motivated permeated the conversation. I pointed out that no one mentioned their hope was an improved test score or improved grades and asked if we should include that in our hope or dream for our kid's future. Unanimously they said no. They wanted more than that for our kids, they wanted them to grow and develop as individuals and learners that weren't just going to be successful on a single assessment but in their life after middle school. That conversation became the foundation for our vision and mission. Taking all the key words and ideas the leadership team and I crafted vision and mission statements and engaged in a process of sending them out the faculty for feedback and revision. The final version was something we all believed in and supported because we were all part of its creation and most importantly it wasn't about test scores or other external things—it was about our kids.

Together we worked to identify our values and our dreams for our students, not for the school per se but for students. We had an idea of what they'd be like when we welcomed them in 6th grade but what would they be like after being with us for three years when they left us in 8th grade? What effect did we hope to have on them and to what end? What was our dream for them? Collaboratively we developed a new vision and new mission for the school that we all agreed reflected who we were as an organization. The vision and mission weren't explicitly or exclusively mine as the principal but were ours as a community. Codified by the new vision and mission faculty, staff, students, parents and the community all worked with commitment to make them reality. The unification of the community around a single vision and mission and use of the statements to guide our work quickly corrected the behavioral issues that had been occurring and recaptured the lost learning time. Teachers and parents could observe the behavioral, social, and academic growth of students. We could see they were learning in all possible ways. As a by-product, and to the pleasure of the school committee and Department of Education, test scores also began to show a positive impact.

No Two Alike

You may have noticed that the practices of the exemplar principals in this book are all slightly different in terms of how instructional leaders engage in their work. In order to be an instructional leader, is it necessary for a principal to be directly involved in the four components of the work of the principal or is it enough that they are indirectly involved? Can their involvement be varied? The simple answer to both of these questions is yes.

Richard Elmore (2000) identified that school leadership is "the guidance and direction of instructional improvement" (p. 13). The idea of providing direction and influence was supported by Leithwood and Riehl's (2003) meta-analysis of school leadership through which they identified that the main function of leadership was to "provide direction and exercise influence" (p. 7). The work of the principal who is an instructional leader must include a focus on learning for students and adults; communicate high expectations for student achievement and instruction; use data to inform the work of the school; and develop a community that is unified around one vision and one mission for the school—but, whether or not principals directly or indirectly engage in these elements does not elevate or disqualify them as an instructional leader. In other words, whether principals are present and actively doing each of the elements themselves is not relevant. What is essential is that they take action to ensure each of the four elements we've identified as the *work* of the principal happens within the school. This suggests that there is no single or "right" way that instructional leaders engage in the *work* of the principal but that each principal may engage in these components based upon the needs of their school and their personal capacity.

Questions for Reflection and Discussion

1. How have you focused on learning in your practice?
2. Whose learning have you focused on? Who might you have overlooked or not focused on as much?
3. Who do you have high expectations for?
4. When and how do you communicate high expectations?
5. What will you accept as evidence that your expectations are being met?
6. How have you used data in your practice? What data have you used?
7. How was the information from the data shared with others in the school?
8. How have you engaged others in the vision and mission of the school?
9. Can students, teachers, and parents explain the vision and mission of the school?
10. Of the four elements of the *work* of the principal, which do you feel you provide the most attention? Why do you feel that element gets more attention than others?
11. Which element would you like to give more attention?
12. Which of the four elements of the *work* of the principal do you feel is a strength in your practice and which do you feel is the weakest? Why?
13. How do you ensure that the areas you are weak in are effectively addressed in your school?
14. How do you enable others to engage in the four elements of the *work* of principals?

References

Bernhardt, V. (2003). *Using data to improve student learning in elementary schools.* Larchmont, NY: Eye on Education.

Carrier, L. and Whaland, M. (2015). *Developing school-wide data teams in small rural schools.* Paper presented at the National Rural Educators Association 107th Convention and Symposium.

Cremin, L. A. (1970). *American Education, the Colonial Experience, 1607–1783.* New York: Harper & Row.

Elmore, R. (2000). *Building a New Structure For School Leadership.* Washington, DC: Albert Shanker Institute.

Feldman, J. and Tung, R. (2001). *Whole school reform: How schools use the data-based inquiry and decision making process.* Paper presented at the Annual Meeting of the American Educational Research Association, Seattle, WA.

Leithwood, K. and Riehl, C. (2003). *What do we already know about successful school leadership?* Paper prepared for the AERA Division A Task Force on Developing Research in Educational Leadership.

Love, N. (2004). Taking data to new depths. *Journal of Staff Development,* 25(4), 22–26.

Merriam-Webster Learner's Dictionary (n.d). Springfield, MA: Merriam-Webster.

NAEP (2015). Retrieved on February 20, 2016 from www.nationsreportcard.gov/reading_math_2015/#?grade=8.

No Child Left Behind Act (2001). P.L. 107–110, sec. 1116 (b) (3).

Noyce, P., Perda, D., and Traver, R. (2000). Creating data-driven schools. *Educational Leadership,* February, 52–56.

Reagan, Ronald (1981). First inaugural address. Retrieved on February 3, 2016 from www.americanrhetoric.com/speeches/ronaldreagandfirstinaugural.html.

Robinson, G., Bursuck, W., and Sinclair, K. (2013). Implementing RTI in two rural elementary schools: Encouraging beginnings and challenges for the future. *The Rural Educator,* 34(3), 1–9.

United States Department of Education. (2009). The American recovery and reinvestment act of 2009: Saving and creating jobs and reforming education. US Department of Education. Retrieved on March 22, 2016 from www2.ed.gov/policy/gen/leg/recovery/implementation.html.

Wormelli, R. (2006). *Fair Isn't Always Equal.* Portland, ME: Stenhouse Publishers.

The Leadership of the Principal

In Chapter 2, we identified a model of instructional leadership that included two big ideas, the *work* of the principal and the *leadership* of the principal. Chapter 3 provided us with a deeper look at the *work* of the principal and how our exemplar instructional leaders ensured the elements of the work were in place in their schools. The awareness that there is not a singular or right way to engage in the *work* of the principal as it relates to being an instructional leader may add to your confusion. It is my fervent hope that it brings some of you relief. As you reflect on your own practice you may now be asking, *but I ensure all of the elements of the work of principals are happening in my school. What do these principals do that is different?* The answer lays in the second word of the instructional leadership construct—*leadership*.

Influenced by the need for principals to meet the demands of high-stakes accountability policies the practice of leadership has been largely replaced by management. As discussed in Chapter 2, this has resulted in a lack of common understanding about the genuine practice of leadership. Key to increasing the clarity between management and leadership is awareness of the quality of the dynamic between leaders and followers. Does the leader understand the needs of the people in their organization? How do they interact with those needs? How do they respond to the needs of those they lead? Lastly, is the relationship between leaders and constituents built on trust? Leaders sincerely care about those they lead at a personal level and are committed to developing a positive relationship with them. This type of human focus can be best described as attending to issues of the heart, a practice particularly essential to the practice of transformative leadership.

Over the course of my research for this book fifty teachers from the schools of the exemplar instructional leaders were interviewed. Twenty-five teachers described their principal as "tak(ing) care of" them and students and "having their backs." They all described that they felt they could trust the principal to look out for their best interest, the best interest of students, and the best interest of the school as a whole. In short, the instructional leaders in the study were perceived as caring about the people in their school's community in what was perceived by the teachers as a real and substantial way. These teachers did not discuss how well a principal analyzed data or to what level they were involved in maintaining a focus on learning when asked about how their principals practiced instructional leadership; but instead described their principals as individuals with whom they had positive, supportive, trust-based relationships.

In 2011, I studied two schools in Massachusetts that were once identified as underperforming by the Commonwealth and turned around to be considered models of professional practice. Principals of these schools were considered by the Commonwealth to be true instructional leaders. What was significant is that the schools were led by the same individuals before, during, and after the turnaround. Not surprisingly the turnaround was not about what the principal did but how they did it. How they engaged in the practice of leadership is what made the difference. Their ability to enable, empower, inspire, protect, and guide were significant to their faculty and provided them the safety and support they needed to look deeply at the achievement issues and related issues of practice that needed to be addressed. Additionally, their willingness to do whatever was necessary to ensure the success of the school was both humbling and inspiring to their faculty and provided them with the model of engagement in the turnaround process they needed. Teachers in these schools never felt isolated or vilified by the process because they were clear that their principal, regardless of whatever else was happening in the district, was in the process with them. These principals, as well as the National Distinguished Principals studied, can all be described through three types of behavior—authentic to self, fearlessness, and personally humble and modest. Although fearlessness and the notion of being humble and modest can be encompassed by the idea of being authentic to self, because of how the importance of each emerged in the practices of our model principals I've included them as separate here.

Authentic to Self

I remember my elementary and junior/senior high school principals; they were both feared and respected. They worked in the dreaded *office* and were rarely seen in the hallways of the school. They came to school each day dressed neatly in suits and sat in their offices managing the school. The school ran like a well-oiled machine. Everyone and everything was where they were supposed to be, when they were supposed to be. Desks were in nice neat rows with students completing their work. Teachers sat or stood in the front or back of the room overseeing that everyone stayed on task. Being sent to the office was beyond dreaded. Although being able to exit high school and enter the work force, military, or secondary education was clearly the goal for all students, it was not the metric by which these principals were measured. The mark of effectiveness was an orderly, safe, clean school where everyone was appropriately engaged in their work. The principals of my childhood were highly respected in the community by virtue of their position; being the school principal carried significant societal status in the 1960s and 1970s. Their decisions were rarely, if ever, questioned by students, parents, or the community and if by teachers it was kept behind the metaphoric wall that separated the school as an organization from the world outside its doors. There was a cultural expectation about the role of principal in those days and principals adopted that persona when they entered into the job.

As I work and speak with principals around the country I have frequently encountered the principal persona. I find myself shocked that for all the educational reform of the last twenty years we still have principals going into schools each day putting on the metaphoric mask they believe represents that persona. Is this a testament to the confusion about the practice of instructional leadership? Is it evidence that as a profession we still don't understand that leadership is an interpersonal dynamic that is founded on the quality of relationships, not one based on station, title, or expected personas? Is it community pressure to conform to a familiar persona of the principal? Or can it simply be the confusion around the practice of leadership itself that causes principals to retreat to a well-known paradigm?

Commonly describing themselves as "I've always been this" or "What you see is what you get," our exemplar instructional leaders did not adopt a perceived role when they entered into a formal school leadership position. They can instead be described as being authentic leaders (Avolio & Gardner,

2005; Gardner, Cogliser, Davis, & Dickens, 2011; Mitchell & Gooty, 2005; Shamir & Eilam, 2005). Each was asked about their transition from teacher to instructional leader. Each of these highly effective principals have been recognized by their professional organization, state departments of education, and/or their peers for their instructional leadership practice but each self-identified they hadn't transitioned into being instructional leaders or into some idealized version of the role of school principal. They did though, with the exception of one, each identify themselves as teachers first and principals second. For them they are first and foremost teachers regardless of what the title may say on their office door. And each identified that they, regardless of their titles or years of service, remained true to themselves; that is, they didn't play a part. These principals didn't morph into the role of principal as an actor might become a character for a play, or don a mask to alter their appearance as one might do for a costume party. These principals remained authentically themselves. In each case the result has been deeply personal, genuine, and mutually supportive relationships with faculty, staff, students, and communities that result in a deep and palpable sense of shared ownership for student achievement.

In order to begin to understand what it means to be an authentic leader we must first have clarity about the meaning of the word authentic as it relates to human behavior and emotion. Returning to the Merriam Webster Learner's Dictionary (n.d), authentic is being "true to one's own personality, spirit, or character." As you reflect on your current reality how would your teachers describe your personality, spirit or character? How would your family or friends describe them? How do you describe them? Is there agreement or would each answer seem to describe a different person?

Found primarily in management research, the study of authentic leadership in the field of education has had minimal attention, giving way to the broader topic areas of transformational and transactional leadership theories (Gardner et al., 2011). In their attempt to bring clarity to the construct of authentic leadership Gardner, Cogliser, Davis, and Dickens (2011) conducted an historical review of the literature analyzing definitions from 1967 to 2009. Examining the evolution of the understanding of how being an authentic leader is understood they identified four central components to the construct—self-awareness, balanced processing, relational transparency, and an internalized moral perspective. Essentially, authentic leaders are aware of who they are as an individual, of who they are emotionally and behaviorally, and of their values. They don't allow their personal values to bias decisions and have empathy for those they lead. To ensure they maintain their objectivity they look outside of themselves to make decisions, carefully considering the potential impact for all those involved. This deliberate action of ensuring objectivity is not intended to delay or avoid action but to ensure that decisions are unbiased and members of the community are treated with equity, fairness, and respect. Authentic leaders are truly transparent in their leadership practice. For them it's not just a matter of making sure targeted outcomes are in the open. Through their sense of moral obligation to ensure that all members of the organization are considered, as much as possible, all decision making processes are fully in the open. Finally, authentic leaders have the moral courage to take action on what is morally right even in the face of what competing external pressures may otherwise deem to be right. Essentially, they walk the walk, they talk regardless of external pressures that may appear. This congruence between words and actions establishes a trust filled environment that supports others in taking risks in their own learning and work (Schminke, Arnaud, & Kuenzi, 2007).

While Gardner et al.'s (2011) components provide a broad look at the construct, Shamir and Eilam's (2005) model provides a more precise perspective that is more easily generalized to the practice of instructional leadership. Subtly different, they operationalize authentic leaders as:

(1) Not acting the part that is perceived to fit the title:

Box 4.1 Voices from Leaders in the Field

Lisa:

Too many times I see new principals come into schools and they think it's about how they look, like it's an image kind of thing. It's not about hundred dollar suits or expensive cars. That stuff makes you inaccessible to your teachers, parents, and kids. It sets the idea that you're way above them socially and they're below you. It can't work that way. We're all in this together. You really have to know a lot about the cultures of your school and be able to make them comfortable. It's getting to know people and breaking down the stereotypes. If you pretend to be some title I'm not sure how you can do that.

(2) Not taking on formal leadership roles for status or notoriety but for reasons of conviction;

> ### Box 4.2 Voices from Leaders in the Field
>
> *Larry:*
>
> Honestly, they don't really tell you in grad school the reality of what you'll do when you take the job. Your training is all about curriculum, supervision, and school law. You think you're coming out and you'll have a title and that means something. No one told me I might be the substitute for a class period because no one else is available, or that I'd be working fourteen hour days because I have an 8:00 am meeting and have to cover the basketball game, that I might need to drive the van to pick up kids for school because the driver was sick, or that I'd need to dry mop the cafeteria floor. I've even put on an apron and gloves and served lunches. The reality is in this job you need to be ready and willing to do whatever needs to be done. There just isn't always enough people and you can't take services from the kids because you don't like to get dirty.

(3) Original and not taking on personas or attempting to become a copy of someone else; and,

> ### Box 4.3 Voices from Leaders in the Field
>
> *Penny:*
>
> When I think about where I learned to do this work I really don't know where. I don't think there's one place or person I can point to and say that's where I learned to be an instructional leader. I think where it's really all come from is my own personal journey in education and in the world outside of it. I've never tried to copy what anyone else does, I have to be me and be true to that so I listen and learn from others and other places. How can I use what they've learned

> to develop myself. I've had practicum students that are looking for a recipe for how to do this. There isn't one you really need to be constantly working on who you are in this role.

(4) Those whose actions are based on values and convictions, not external pressures.

> **Box 4.4 Voices from Leaders in the Field**
>
> *Helen:*
>
> I really believe in the idea of leadership by example and never asking more of my staff than I'm willing to do myself. They see that if nothing else I have a good work ethic. Maybe it was my background growing up. My mom was a teacher, my dad was an electrician. You know my parents taught me this whole value of hard work.

What is clear from the practices of our exemplar instructional leaders is that they can each be described as having authentic and transformative leadership practices. It is worth noting here that transformational leaders can also be described as inauthentic. While those leaders may generate a culture of compliance they are less likely to be effective in the long term, as it's unlikely they'll create the environment necessary for sustainability of efforts (Hargreaves & Fink, 2006). The work of our exemplar principals begs the question, if we're going to truly develop our schools to meet the needs of all our students in the 21st century is it time that we, as school leaders, drop any personas we may have adopted and be our authentic selves?

Fearlessness

Collins (2001) described his level 5 leaders as having a "ferocious resolve" (p. 18) to do whatever is necessary for the success of the organization. In the case of school principals those that are practicing instructional leadership at this same level can best be described as *fearless*. For these leaders, their priority above all else is the school, the people in it, and the overall success of the organization. They don't allow external pressures, personal or professional, to dissuade them from staying true to their beliefs and convictions regardless of the potential peril to their own self-interests that may establish.

This sense of fearlessness is true of all our exemplar principals. Regardless of the grade level of their school or accolades they've received, all can be described as driven in their personal resolve to ensure that their school is successful in making sure every learner in the school community achieves at the highest level possible. They will do whatever they feel they must do to make that vision a reality. The fearlessness of principals was described by teachers in each case as the principal making some form of personal or professional sacrifice to ensure the success of the school.

Box 4.5 *Voices from Leaders in the Field*

Terry:

It was the teachers that said, "What can we do?" They all agreed to all these changes. It was my job to fight with central office. Central office was all Math Investigations; we were Singapore Math. Teachers here said we're going to do Singapore. In a way you gotta be a rebel if you want to change. But it was my teachers that said this is what we gotta do. The teachers will tell you why the scores went up; it wasn't necessarily me as it was what was done. I did battle with Central Office over it and we got Singapore so now they make things hard for me downtown but Singapore is working for our kids so it was worth it.

Reading Coordinator about Lisa:

She's not afraid to say what she thinks. It's not about pleasing parents; she's about what's best for children. Whether or not you agree, she's still going to say it and back it up with why. Not a lot of people in leadership like that. They play the "how can I make you happy" game.

Box 4.6 Voices from Leaders in the Field

Third Grade Teacher about Terry:

He admits he is not the educator of the reading, math, and things like that. He'll say, "I haven't taught children how to read. You know how to teach them to read. What do you think?" He does a lot of that. He gets a lot of flack for that. I think it's because he has the courage to do that. I think that in other places there are administrators who don't do that. They're like puppets on a string. They are more concerned with listening to what the people above them say, than to the people in the buildings working with kids.

English Teacher about Bob:

Oh my gosh he gives up so much personally to make sure that we have what we need for the kids. He's here before all of us, and we get here at 7:00 am. He's here after most people leave too. I've been here at four and five o'clock working with the drama club kids and he's still here. Then he'll be here at night for sports events, he never misses them, school board meetings, PTA, or sports booster meetings. He easily works 12–14 hours most days and I'm sure he never works an eight hour day during the school year. I'm not sure when he actually sees his family. The amount of time and energy he gives us here is so immense I can't imagine what he has left for them. And the thing is it's not because he has to, no one tells him to. He just feels it's really important that as the leader he's involved in the community type things in a real way and that he's here working with all of us. It makes a difference too. If we need something the community supports us every time. It's because he's involved. If he needs something from all of us we do it. But it costs him personally.

All sacrificed in their own way, but teachers agree that the sacrifice was personal, and that they placed the school beyond their own needs and ambitions. They additionally agreed that the level of resolve displayed served as a model and source of inspiration for how they engaged in their own work.

> **Box 4.7 Voices from Leaders in the Field**
>
> *Special Education Teacher about Lisa:*
>
> I'm in awe of her. She bought all those boots [reference to three dozen pairs of winter boots on storage shelves] with her money. These are winter boots for kids that don't have boots. So what she does is, scope it out, sees who doesn't have boots for the season. She gives them boots for the season; when they're done they bring them back. Every year Walmart has a big sale, every year she buys boots. She makes sure every kid has a coat. There's a rack, her mother and her do all the scarves, hats, and mittens—they're not for them to take home but to use here. They fold them up and put them back on the rack. But every kid goes outside with warm clothes. She's just such a great role model for us of what it means to be an educator.

Constantly identifying that they were "in awe" and "inspired," teachers that work under the leadership of these principals find themselves engaging in behaviors and activities at the school they may not otherwise have done.

> I also think I wouldn't have been pushed so hard professionally to be the best that I can be if it wasn't for working in this school. Now because of Lisa, because we're a Compass School, I have other schools, other school systems coming in to look at me, to watch me teach. Because of her, I'm able to teach other special education teachers and speech and language pathologists in the district how to teach some of my programs. I would never have put myself out there if it wasn't for her. She makes me want to take the risk to be a better teacher. I think that on a personal level we all take care of each other and on a professional level we all push each other to be our best. It's because of her.

Personally Humble and Modest

Collins (2001) described his Level 5 leaders as "a study in duality" (p. 22). In the context of instructional leadership I am in total agreement with him. In counterbalance to the trait of fearlessness, these leaders are also personally humble and modest. Instructional leaders do not make themselves the centerpiece of the school but instead make the school and those they lead the focus. This is true of each of the exemplar instructional leaders. Each takes no credit for the success of their school but instead attributes the successes to their teachers. In each case the principals shared that they felt it was nothing they had done—that it was the work of the teachers that made the difference. Ironically, the teachers in all cases agreed that they could not have done the work they did were it not for their principals empowering them to do so and protecting them from influences that could potentially minimize that empowerment.

A by-product of the humility and modesty of these principals is a true model of shared leadership. The development of the professional community into a shared leadership model unifies schools around a single vision and mission. Vision and mission aren't forced upon members but instead they are able to interact with them, entrusted and empowered to act in service to their realization. A teacher at one school described it this way,

> We never feel he's an administrator who disregards what we have to say or think and simply mandates initiatives. He trusts and respects our ability implicitly. So he pretty much without exception lets us take the reins.

Box 4.8 Voices from Leaders in the Field

Lisa:

A piece of it for a principal is not having to deal with every issue. I think this is key—I think that some principals, and I think I was probably guilty of it as a newer principal, feel like they have to be in on every single piece of it or you're losing control of it. But you don't. You have to be in on the big picture and see the big picture, and let those people around you make those decisions and live with them.

Box 4.9 Voices from Leaders in the Field

Science Teacher about Bob:

We all have a voice in everything. It's just that simple. He works closely with the leadership team and they represent all of us. They bring stuff back to us and stuff from us to him. If something new is happening he makes sure the leadership team brings it back to all of us and gets our feedback and input. Then they consolidate it all so we can see it during faculty meetings and we have whole faculty conversations. I think because of that in particular we all have taken ownership of what happens here. It's not my classroom or your classroom it's our school and our kids. We all roll up our sleeves no matter what it is. I really do think that's because he's created a system and communication channel that really shares his leadership with all of us.

As was observed by all of the principals, teachers experienced their humility and modesty as a sign of trust and respect for them personally and professionally. The confidence that this engendered not only inspired the teachers to actively engage in shared leadership but supported them in staying engaged. In short, because teachers weren't considered passive participants waiting for direction they instead became actively engaged in the vision and mission and personally invested in their realization.

How Can I Develop My Leadership?

Practitioners who may be reading this will no doubt ask, *if I don't possess these traits can I develop them?* Collins (2001) hypothesizes that potential leaders have the ability to evolve into level 5 or in the case of school principals, instructional leaders with a holistic practice. There is no formula for how to develop these traits: if Collins's (2001) hypothesis is correct, the traits are in some ways inherent in that there is some starting point for the behavior to be developed from. In contrast, commonly accepted beliefs of human psychology regarding the ability of humans to learn and unlearn behaviors suggest that the ability to learn behaviors that demonstrate the qualities of these traits is possible. Whether you're at a point of needing to evolve existing behaviors or learning new ones, the targeted leadership behaviors discussed can be explored and brought forward in practice through the process of mindfulness, personal reflection, and coaching.

Mindfulness

We are more and more aware of the benefits of being mindful in our day to day living; but, in an educational environment overrun with the continuous bombardment of external and internal demands is it possible to practice mindfulness in order to develop our leadership practice? Jon Kabat-Zinn (1990) defines mindfulness as,

> ... purposefully paying attention to things we ordinarily never give a moment's thought to. It is a systematic approach to developing new kinds of control and wisdom in our lives, based on our inner capacities for relaxation, paying attention, awareness, and insight.
>
> (p. 2)

It is easy to imagine in the day-to-day life of today's school principal why they may struggle to relax or pay attention to the seemingly ordinary. Between student issues, parent concerns, central office demands, competing policy and regulatory requirements, and teacher issues the constant and often multifaceted demands on a principal's time and energy can inhibit attention to the comparatively less obviously urgent details (Shamir & Eilam, 2005; Van der Merwe & Parsotam, 2011). However, Fiol and O'Connor (2003) remind us that by not practicing some level of mindfulness we run the risk of moving into a potentially inauthentic state; and subsequently assuming a leadership persona, weakening the potential effectiveness of our leadership.

While many people today practice mindfulness for the purposes of health and well-being, the way in which the principals discussed in this book practice mindfulness is different in that it is focused on their own practice as a means of ensuring organizational health and the overall well-being of those within the school community. By being vigilant about checking in with how well they are staying true to their sense of self as they move through each day and week they are able to develop, nourish, and maintain trust-based relationships with their constituents, relationships necessary to ensure sustained engagement of the community with the vision and mission of the school (Zhu, Avolio, Riggio, & Soski, 2011). Each of the exemplar instructional leaders have, as Weik and Sutcliffe (2006) described, "... a clear comprehension of emerging threats and on factors that interfere with such comprehension" (p. 516). In other words, if they threw a rock into a pond they would look carefully to see where each ripple ends, which edges of the shoreline are affected, and which are not. Most importantly they take the time to thoughtfully observe how each ripple affects the next and the way in which

---

Box 4.10 Voices from Leaders in the Field

Bonnie:

After we put what we thought were the big structures in place that would make a difference we kept spinning out data and we found that they didn't make the difference we hoped. We had to step back and not look just at the numbers but at the kids as a whole. What were all the pieces that influenced them? Ya know what they couldn't read. That was the real issue. We had big tough kids that would do just horrible things all because they didn't want anyone to know they couldn't read. So I knew when I was taking over as the principal that I needed to flip the entire model. The stand and deliver, teacher in front of the room, traditional model for teaching 5th and 6th grade wasn't working. The kids couldn't read! So we went to guided reading and small group instruction. Teachers started to realize, if we taught them on their level we could move them forward and that everyone felt safe and secure. We did what felt like 50 million different things but it wasn't until we stopped focusing on test scores and took the time to reflect on all the pieces that we were able to get to the real issue and make a difference for everyone in the school.

they together affect the shoreline. While this analogy may seem simplistic, a practice of mindfulness that supports the development of healthy organizations is a process of thinking deeply about internal and external demands and influences, how each affects the other and the people in the organization, and ultimately how each supports the realization of the

> **Box 4.11 Voices from Leaders in the Field**
>
> *Lisa:*
> We really worked to get all the parents involved in their kid's education however they were able but we knew we were missing some. We were frustrated. Everyone was working hard and there was a group of parents that weren't getting involved the way we thought they should. That was really the key—the way *we* thought they should. They [students] were talking about going to visit their father or mother, and they'd say, "In that place, ya know, it's brick, and there's bricks inside, and ya have to go through that thing that buzzes." Finally it hit me they were at the jail. I finally realized if they [parents] can't come to me, then I gotta go to them. We had a relationship with the jail on another level. Guards that came in did the GEAR thing, kind of like DARE[2] with the guards. I called them and said is there any way I can go in and talk to them [parents] and can I bring somebody with me. So I brought another parent with me and we were very non-judgmental, and we worked on what can we do to help you have better relationship with your child while you're here so they can be successful. We could have just assumed the parents didn't want to be involved but once I really listened it all made sense and we could get to them. It wasn't about how we thought they should be involved it was about understanding how they could be involved and helping them do that.
>
> 1 GEAR is a gang education and resistance program that was provided by the county Sheriff's Department to county schools through a Safe and Drug Free Schools Grant.
> 2 DARE is a drug and alcohol resistance education program that is provided by local police departments to schools.

unified vision and mission of the school. While it is unlikely that any of the principals discussed in this book ever felt they relaxed, they did pay attention to, maintain awareness of, and develop insights about the needs of their constituents and their own leadership practices.

Personal Reflection

It has become commonly accepted that teachers should engage in reflective practice in order to develop their craft. In many schools it has been established as an expectation that teachers demonstrate in some way that they've reflected on lessons and used what they learn from that process to refine their practice. But what about school leaders, has reflective practice truly been established as an expectation for them? School leaders as professionals often share that they'd like to spend time reflecting on their practice but in their day to day life are unable to find the time to do so. The continual and diverse demands on their time, attention, and energy leave them feeling they do not have the necessary personal resources to spend on reflection. But what if they did? How might that begin to change their day-to-day experience? How might that affect their practice of leadership? Researchers on authentic leadership would likely argue that the practice of reflection could substantially alter the day to day experience of principals as it would facilitate the development and maintenance of authenticity (Avolio & Gardner, 2005).

For our exemplary instructional leaders the practice of personal reflection is not necessarily a structured formal activity. They do however take time each week to reflect on how things are going at the school generally, particular events, how they are doing personally, and how their behavior has influenced others during the week. While some chose to keep this as a solely private experience others chose to include constituents in their reflective processes through the active seeking of feedback and engagement in collegial discourse. Although not a chosen format by our model instructional leaders, there are more and more principals in the field utilizing blogs and other forms of social media to expand their collegial discourse beyond their local circle.

In addition to reflecting on the immediate issues of practice that emerge during a given day or week, the practice of reflection can develop authentic leadership through the construction of personal narratives

Box 4.12 Voices from Leaders in the Field

Penny:

As the leader I feel like it's important to always see my part in things. Not just who I am as "the boss" but how do I influence the people and situations. When I went through my licensure program they had us write reflections and keep journals about how we were developing our practice. When I first got the job I thought that would be a good thing to keep doing. Then reality hit. The day is so crazy sometimes that I just couldn't find the time and when I did find the time I felt guilty for taking it. I started to realize that taking the time to work on me that way was beneficial for everyone else! [Laughed] Even though I don't write things down I make sure I take an hour every Friday afternoon after the kids leave. I walk the halls. I walk around the perimeter of the grounds. Everyone is gone and it's quiet. I spend the time immersed in the building and grounds and I reflect on the week. What went well? What didn't? What influence did I have in any of it or in anything I see on my walk? It's really helped me to develop my practice because I'm thinking about my practice not just doing it.

Bob:

I make sure that I meet with my assistant principal every week, either Monday morning or Friday afternoon. We just check in with each other on things we've handled and talk about how it went. What could we have done differently, that kind of thing. It's really our time to make sure we're being the type of leader we hope we are and if we fall off, that's our time to get back on board.

(Shamir & Eilam, 2005; Sparrow, 2005). Frequently, we are called upon to recount our personal narratives in interviews for employment but less often do we take the time to reflect on our personal narrative as a mechanism for developing our awareness of self, our values, our convictions, and how they each came to be. The construction of our personal narratives is in itself a complex task to be sure. "The employment of the

> Blogs:
>
> A Principal's Reflections
> http://esheninger.blogspot.com/
>
> Lead Learner, Elementary School Principal, otherwise known as PrincipalJ
> http://www.principalj.net/
>
> Reflections of a First Year Principal
> https://inwoodacademyblog.org/2014/08/11/reflections-of-a-first-year-principal/
>
> LinkedIn Groups:
>
> Great Schools: Instructional Leadership Coaching and Development
> National Association of Elementary School Principals
> National Association of Secondary School Principals
> Principals, School Directors, Deans, and Educational Leaders
>
> Twitter Handles to Follow:
>
> National Association of Elementary School Principals @NAESP
> National Association of Secondary School Principals @NASSP
>
> Twitter Hashtags to Watch:
>
> #PrincipalPLN , #Pricipalchat, #EWChat

Figure 4.1 Examples of Social Media Sources for Expanding Collegial Discourse

self is not a process of winnowing what is distinctively one's own from all that surrounds one; instead, it is a process of crafting a distinctive plot through which one's own character takes shape" (Sparrow, 2005, p. 431). The combination of facts and moments of fiction that emerge in response to how we personally make sense of or experience or an event can complicate the development of our narrative. As Shamir and Eilam (2005) point out, the construction of personal narrative is not about creating an announcement of accomplishments but recounting events and people and making sense of the lessons learned from the experiences. Awareness of our personal narrative as leaders provides us with a clearer self-concept

Box 4.13 Voices from Leaders in the Field

Helen:

I believe happy people work hard. It's more than working hard though. Whether your 18 or 80 it's about having a goal and purpose in your life. I also believe you have to lead by example. I think I got those things from my Dad. My Dad grew up in a home where there was poverty. He was a self-made man. He became a master electrician, got a business degree, he had his own business. Despite growing up in poverty he became very successful. But in another family, I think he may have been a lawyer. He said that's what he always wanted to be but he dropped out of school and joined the army and got his GED. He went to business school. He was the guy when he got home from work his first question to us was, "what did you accomplish today?" My mother would ask, "how was your day sweetheart?" but him he wanted to know what we accomplished. I remember the first time he asked. I didn't know what he meant. He said, "What did you get done? I hope you got something done today. A whole day went by." He accomplished something every day and wanted to make sure we did too. So then I'd have to have a list every day. I remember as a teenager thinking, what am I going to tell my father? Even now, I make sure at the end of every day I have something I can tell him I accomplished. The work we do is hard but there's nothing more important we can do in the big world.

and a clear understanding of how we understand leadership and followership, allowing us to effectively engage in our leadership roles.

Coaching

We all likely have experienced some type of coaching experience. Whether through the experience of organized sports, music lessons, or the guided practice provided by a teacher, we have all in some way known the receipt of feedback for our performance on a skill or group of skills with guidance on how to improve. Although in the moment we may not have been enamored with the experience, reflecting on those coaching moments, we see the value of that type of learning and have in many ways sought to replicate it in our classrooms. Instructional strategies and designs like guided practice and the workshop model are considered to be *best practices* in the pk-12 world of education due to their ability to provide coaching for learners.

In the field of education it is becoming a common practice for schools to employ instructional coaches—personnel charged with providing feedback and support for the improvement of the instructional practice of teachers. Instructional coaches typically have expertise in a particular content area and focus their coaching on that particular area of the curriculum. Key to the coaching relationship is that it is confidential, thus providing a safe learning environment for the teachers. Less often witnessed in practice is coaching for school leaders.[1] As Lochmiller (2014) noted, coaching for school leaders unlike teachers focuses on more than practice within the context of one particular period of time but also focuses on the individual and the organization as it exists around them. Through a strong coaching relationship, principals are able to examine their instructional

---

Box 4.14 *Voices from Leaders in the Field*

Larry:

As a new principal I think the best thing the district did for me was allow me to have a coach. He wasn't just some guy that had been retired, I know a lot of people get that, he was trained in coaching and had been a successful high school principal himself. He knew the role, understood the types of challenges I might face. At first he came every week and we'd spend some part of the morning checking in. It was my time so he let me direct what I wanted to talk to him about. Whatever it was he'd help me process it and see all the different sides of things. Then we might do a walk through or meet with a group of teachers together. We'd talk about what I was seeing and hearing. It was so beneficial in helping me move into the role. After all these years I still call him up.

> **Box 4.15 Voices from Leaders in the Field**
>
> *Terry:*
>
> We're successful because of what teachers did, it's not anything I did, and I mean that. Looking out for the teachers is my job—it's what I'm supposed to do. I have a mentor through NISL, he asks me what my legacy will be here. I tell him I honestly don't know and you know what? —I don't. But it's something I'm thinking about and he'll help me think about and I know he'll help me to understand.

leadership practice holistically through the support of a confidential coaching relationship with an individual with expertise and experience in the role of school leader. Coaching supports the leader in developing their awareness of self and how they interact with their constituents and the school organization as a whole. In that way coaching becomes an ideal vehicle for the development and maintenance of an authentic leadership practice.

Questions for Reflection and Discussion

1. How did you experience the principals of your childhood?
2. How do you describe the principal persona? What do they look and sound like? What do they do?
3. Why did you become (or do you want to become) a school principal?
4. What personal values and convictions do you bring to the leadership role?
5. What is important to you?
6. What are your personal strengths and weaknesses?
7. What are you passionate about?
8. How do you react to perceived resistance to your ideas or decisions?
9. How does how you've engaged in the role of school principal align with your sense of self?

10. What is your personal narrative?
11. How has your personal narrative contributed to who you've become as a school leader?

Note

1 Because of the nature of work being done it is not uncommon for coaching and mentoring to be used interchangeably in the field.

References

Avolio, B. and Gardner, W. (2005). Authentic leadership development: Getting to the root of positive forms of leadership. *The Leadership Quarterly*, (16), 315–338.

Collins, J. (2001). *Good to Great*. New York: HarperCollins.

Fiol, C. M. and O'Connor, E. J. (2003). Waking up! Mindfulness in the face of bandwagons. *Academy of Management Review*, 28(1), 54–70.

Gardner, W., Cogliser, C., Davis, K., and Dickens, P. (2011). Authentic leadership: A review of the literature and research agenda. *The Leadership Quarterly*, (22), 1120–1145.

Hargreaves, A. and Fink, D. (2006). *Sustainable Leadership*. San Francisco, CA: Jossey-Bass.

Kabat-Zinn, J. (1990). *Full Catastrophe Living*. New York: Delacorte Press.

Lochmiller, C. (2014). Leadership coaching in an induction program for novice principals: A 3-year study. *Journal of Research on Leadership Education*, 9(1), 59–84.

Mitchell, S. and Gooty, J. (2005). Values, emotions, and authenticity: Will the real leaders please stand up? *The Leadership Quarterly*, (16), 441–457.

Schminke, M., Arnaud, A., and Kuenzi, M. (2007). The power of ethical work climates. *Organizational Dynamics*, 36(2), 171–186.

Shamir, B. and Eilam, G. (2005). What's your story? A life-stories approach to authentic leadership development. *The Leadership Quarterly*, (16), 395–417.

Sparrow, T. (2005). Authentic leadership and narrative self. *The Leadership Quarterly*, (16), 419–439.

Van der Merwe, H. and Parsotam, A. (2011). School principal stressors and a stress alleviation strategy based on controlled breathing. *Journal of Asian and African Studies*, 47(6), 666–678.

Weik, K. and Sutcliffe, K. (2006). Mindfulness and the quality of organizational attention. *Organization Science*, 17(4), 514–524.

Zhu, W., Avolio, B., Riggio, R., and Soski, J. (2011). The effect of authentic transformational leadership on follower and group ethics. *Leadership Quarterly*, 22, 801–817.

5 | Overcoming Perceived Barriers

Now that we're clear that the practice of instructional leadership is a richer more robust form of leadership practice that moves beyond the simple *to do list* of the day, it's time to move our attention to developing our individual practices. Specifically to developing our practice of instructional leadership as holistic, that is it not only includes the *work* of principals but

The work of the principal	The leadership of the principal  Instructional Leadership
• focuses on learning for students and adults • communicates high expectations for student achievement and instruction • uses data to inform the work of the school • develops a community that is unified around one vision and one mission for the school	• is authentic • includes behaviors that demonstrate fearlessness • includes behaviors that demonstrate personal modesty and humility

Figure 5.1 A Holistic Model of Instructional Leadership

it also includes an *authentic and transformative leadership* practice. As you reflect on the previous chapters and your existing practice of instructional leadership you may feel that your practice is more developed than you had originally thought. Perhaps you are beginning to see points of practice that you can further develop. Maybe you're beginning to identify some obstacles that you'll need to navigate in order to move forward. Or perhaps, and I hope this will not be the case for many, you feel that while you now understand the practice of instructional leadership the barriers to developing your practice seem so insurmountable that you don't feel you can move forward. It is for you that we will explore potential barriers with hopes that you'll begin to see ways to overcome them.

Personal Vision and Mission

Before we begin to identify and explore the commonly identified barriers to developing the practice of instructional leadership, let's first ground ourselves in why we entered into the field of educational leadership in the first place. Just like our schools have vision and mission statements to guide decision making and unify communities, we too have vision and missions as individual leaders. Often unspoken, our personal vision and mission encapsulates our hopes, goals, and dreams for the future and our plans for making that future a reality. Consider this quote from Henry Ford, "... When I'm through, everyone will be able to afford one, and everyone will have one. The horse will disappear from the highways, the automobile will be taken for granted . . ." (Adams, 1993). Certainly there were a variety of obstacles that may have prevented him from utilizing the assembly line for the mass production of what was then considered affordable automobiles. His vision is what allowed him to continuously measure his progress toward the future he dreamed of, what guided him in developing new strategies to ensure he got there, and what supported him in educating others in what his view of the future could be. Returning to why we chose to be a school principal puts us in touch with our personal vision and mission and provides us with a guidepost to measure our practice against.

In 1998, when I made the decision to enter into the field of educational leadership, the standards-based reform movement in Massachusetts was just getting started in our district. I could see the possibilities for standards-based instruction and how it could be an opportunity for richer more robust learning opportunities for students. The days of rote learning and skill and drill were moving behind us and the opportunity for learners of all ages to engage in the natural process of inquiry to really engage in deep learning was upon us. In this new educational environment learning would no longer be compartmentalized into discrete subject areas but could be an integrated process through which the skills from Mathematics, Social Studies, the Arts, and English Language Arts could find synergy and become more obviously relevant to students. In that new educational paradigm students would be able to exit school prepared for the demands of their future as opposed to prepared to meet the demands of our past. That was my vision for the future of education. Everyone around me saw it as well. The field of education was changing. Sadly, I started to observe massive points of resistance that were slowing and in some cases preventing the type of learning environment I was envisioning from becoming reality. It was then that my mission emerged, *to create the kind of school I wanted for my own children.* That's when I made the decision to enter into the field of educational leadership. Beginning with my leadership role as an assistant principal, all my decision making was measured against a simple question: W*hat would I want if this were my child?*

Box 5.1 Voices from Leaders in the Field

Larry:

When I first started in administration I got asked that all the time. What's your vision for the school? I always kind of pull back from it because to me it's not my vision it's *our* vision. If it's just about me what happens if I can't be here for some reason? So I started asking back, what do we want for our kids here?

That really is my personal vision, that we as a community committed to kids have a collective vision for them that we agree on, that the kids are ours, not yours, not mine but ours. When I stop to think about that I believe that has made a tremendous difference in our school, the idea that it's *ours.* Even on the most difficult days it's knowing that we all share in the ownership of what happens for and with these kids that makes the biggest difference.

In each of my Principal Practicum Seminar courses I ask students to develop their personal vision and mission statements. More than meeting a course requirement, their awareness of their personal vision and mission helps them to develop a sense of who they are as aspiring leaders, who they want to be when they enter into the role, and perhaps more importantly why they want to become school principals. What is common across the statements of my students is that none say they want to become a school principal to ensure test scores go up or to ensure that everyone teaches the same way on the same day. They instead talk about creating schools that support all learners in the process of learning—learning about themselves, the world, and all the possibilities within each. What is also common among my students is a concern about their ability to realize their visions because of the types of barriers they observe in the field. In particular they identify policy pressures and community expectations as negatively influencing the ability of their mentor principals to engage in a holistic practice of instructional leadership. Sadly, the barriers they see are the same ones I faced myself during my career and why we need to be transparent about exploring them today. It's only through open and candid dialogue that the persistent barriers to practice, both real and perceived, can be overcome.

Potential Barriers to Developing a Holistic Practice of Instructional Leadership

The Positive and Negative Impacts of Policy

A potential and often cited barrier to the development of a holistic practice of instructional leadership is the very policies that dictate the need for the practice (Jimerson, 2005). At the most basic level the intention of all policies is to control human behavior for the benefit of the general welfare of the population. Just as all policies do, educational policies have the intended consequence of correcting or preventing some issue that is identified as having a potential negative impact on the community or some portion of it. Policies like *A Nation at Risk* (1983), the No Child Left Behind Act (2001), and the Race to the Top Act (2009) link education to the potential economic success of the country and identify a need to improve schooling to ensure that success. In service to that mission the federal reform policies of the last twenty years focused on two key issues—accountability and the evaluation of educators as mechanisms for improving student achievement (Coburn, Hill, & Spillane, 2016).

As pointed out by Rallis and MacMullen (2000), the external accountability approaches of the late 1990s didn't carry with them a process of developing the internal capacities of schools to implement them. Although the reform policies of the early 21st century included provisions for educators to develop both instructional *and* leadership capacities, they did not operationalize leadership. They failed to explicitly specify that the practice of instructional leadership includes leadership practices and behaviors not just the tangible tasks of the job (NCLB, 2001; US Department of Education, 2009). The underlying belief of these reform polices has been that the threat of negative consequences and promise of rewards is sufficient to incite improvement in student achievement through improvement in instructional and (what the policies refer to as) leadership abilities. The result has been an external focus on accountability instead of an internal focus on the development of professional practice, contributing to the frequent lack of sustainability of policy initiatives that occurs in schools (Hargreaves & Fink, 2006). Combined with the rapid changes in policy, this outward compliance oriented focus is prohibitive to the deep and authentic development of a holistic practice of instructional leadership. Subsequently, implementation of educational policies often has had the unintended consequence of moving leadership to the practice of management under the guise of leadership.

While there are clearly some prohibitive factors to these educational policies there are also some supportive factors. The policies of the last twenty years have for the first time defined the *work* of principals. Under these policies the image portrayed by the *Man in the Corner Office* is no longer acceptable. The administrator in suit and tie sitting behind closed doors at their desk removed from the learning process, managing the day to day business functions, and only intervening on issues deemed critical has become by virtue of policy demands obsolete. The advent of the standards-based reform movement in the late 1990s required that all of us as educators, including principals, focus on learning in a new way. No longer is the classroom considered the sole domain of teachers but in order to understand, manage, and hopefully lead what is happening educationally in a school, principals need to be in classrooms observing teaching and learning beyond the obligatory annual evaluation observation. Principals

Overcoming Perceived Barriers

> I once had a job in a place where men
> wore ties. The ties were silk, not wool,
> and my collar was crisp and white.
> I was the man in the corner office. It was
> larger than the others' and bright with sun.
> My window flowers bloomed and
> people did my bidding. My leather chair
> had arms, but I was never fooled.
> I knew my only life was being sold
> for gold, no different in that regard
> from the secretary who brought my
> morning coffee, the maid who mopped
> the men's room floor, the copy guy,
> and all the rest.

Figure 5.2 The Man in the Corner Office
Source: Rossiter, 2014, p. 155

for the first time in the history of public education in the United States are expected to know how all students in the school, not just the elite few that are considered *above average*, are progressing toward meeting the identified curriculum standards. For all the ways that policy can prohibit the development of a holistic practice of instructional leadership we would be remiss as a profession not to acknowledge that without these policies we may not even be having the conversation about how to effectively practice instructional leadership.

Accountability Policy

The accountability policies of the late 1990s and early part of the 21st century are predicated on a reward and punishment mentality. Through them schools and potentially the educators in them are rewarded for student success on state tests of literacy, mathematics, and science and are punished for low levels of success on the same tests. NCLB (2001) legislation required that *all* students reach proficiency by 2014 on literacy and mathematics testing. Eight years later RttT (2009) policy writers amended the proficiency goal to all achievement gaps on high-stakes testing closed by half by 2016. Although they may look different from state to state, schools not meeting required identified progress toward goals under these policies received sanctions through the declaration that they were underperforming. Identification as underperforming carried with it requirements for schools that included a potentially high level of intervention from the state such as the ability for parents to move their children to schools that were not identified as underperforming, the removal of educators, state take over, and the potential closing of schools.

In response to NCLB (2001) an identified need emerged in districts for what became known as *turnaround* of underperforming schools resulting in the common practice of school principals receiving short, most often year-to-year contracts. Principals were expected to show improvement on their school's state test scores in a year and in each year they were subsequently employed at the school. In this way although it had not yet become formally a part of the evaluation process through policy, in practice student test scores became used for the purpose of making hiring decisions. *Change agents*, or principals that would come in and engage in quick fix solutions became highly sought after during the NCLB era of education. The mission of *change agents* was to quickly turnaround the school in order to avoid further policy sanctions—to move it from underperforming to performing, with continued employment being predicated on their progress in meeting that directive. Lacking in the time necessary for the development of the culture necessary for sustainability of new practices, the practice of engaging in short turnarounds flies in the face of what we know from research about the change process and of what we know about the holistic practice of instructional leadership (Carrier, 2011; Fullan, 2001; Hargreaves & Fink, 2006). As a result the vast majority of initiatives implemented under *change agents* only lasted for the tenure of the principal and many of the schools that had been labeled as underperforming remained so under the policies of the time.

As Jim Spillane (2006) identified, the myopic punitively driven focus on improving test scores undermines the quality of education for students. The consequences of our cultural refocusing on achievement as measured by state tests as opposed to learning and then achievement can be seen in the latest NAEP data (NAEP, 2015). The focus on test scores has also undermined the practice of leadership, requiring us instead to become managers. As discussed in Chapter 2, principals in the field have shared they feel they are less able to engage in leadership behaviors because of the amount of time they need to spend on management and ensuring compliance on policy driven initiatives. Have the policies taken that time from us as a profession or is it our perception?

As Spillane also pointed out, in a system that's founded on a reward and punishment model a culture of fear develops—for students fear of not doing well on *the test* and not being promoted to the next grade level, of losing their teacher or school; for teachers fear of job loss and reputation because students didn't do well enough on *the test*; for principals fear of job loss and reputation because the school didn't do well enough on *the test*; for central office administration fear of job loss and reputation because the schools in the district didn't do well on *the test*. For the role

---

Box 5.2 Voices from Leaders in the Field

Terry:

They [teachers] saw the problem, and they said how we're going to tackle it. We knew we were going to cross paths with central office on some issues like Title 1. They said we couldn't pull from kindergarten. I said we were. And you know they're right because it catches up. But we saw the need to do something, and we did it.

Penny:

Ya know what it's about the kids and what do they need to be successful. Those test scores we get back from the state are all well and fine. We have to do them and they'll use them how they need to and so will we. We look at the whole student and come up with what we think will best help them to grow. The Curriculum Director doesn't always agree with me but that's fine we're going to do what we think is best for kids regardless of a single test score. You really have to be willing and able to speak your mind, back it up with the research on instructional practices, and the variety of data you have and be willing to keep speaking up for your kids.

Box 5.3 Voices from Leaders in the Field

Doug:

What is the end goal? Let's agree on the end before we go through the process. So there's certain things in education we have to do. For example, during the *No Child Left Behind* years you had to have at the end of the day kids being able to demonstrate their knowledge in a certain kind of environment. You don't have to agree with the environment, it's required so we have to do it but that doesn't mean skill and drill and teaching them how to bubble. It does mean at the end of the day we need kids to be able to demonstrate what they know in a particular environment. That doesn't mean that's it and we can't do project-based learning. That doesn't mean we abandon our vision and philosophy. That means we look to see how we can make those required things fit into what we do.

Bob:

Every time the high-stakes test score conversation comes up and what should be done to raise test scores for particular groups I ask my teachers what's the purpose of what we do. At first they looked confused but now they tell me, to educate them for their future not our past. That's what it's all about. All the tests and assessments are fine and we get some really valuable information from them about our kids but if we're designing and delivering curriculum with 21st century learning in mind we've failed our kids if we just focus on test scores. We simply can't abandon authentic relevant learning experiences so we can practice for the test. Doing great on a single test on a single day isn't going to help our students develop the thinking, communication, collaborative, and high level academic skills they need to be successful in their life time. They just give us a little information that we can add to all the curriculum embedded performance assessments we do and all the other project-based and real learning that happens here.

of principal this fear driven culture has frequently contributed to rapid turnover of school principals and the adoption of practices and behaviors that are less than educationally sound or professionally acceptable (Hargreaves & Fink, 2006). In extreme cases this sense of fear has been the motivator for principals to cheat on state tests. For most principals however, the punishment portion of accountability has resulted in a refocusing of their time away from the practice of leadership and toward a practice of management. Concerned that they'll be deemed ineffective because of state test scores, they spend their time getting a set of prescribed tasks completed, making sure teachers are doing everything that has been mandated through policy and by central office administration.

How then did some principals successfully engage in a holistic practice of instructional leadership under these policies? All public schools and subsequently their principals are bound by accountability policies and face the same potential consequences for failure to show progress toward the identified proficiency goals. In the case of our exemplar principals it was a matter of staying true to themselves and their beliefs. While they acknowledged the need for the school to reflect on the mission set out by policies, they didn't succumb to personal fears but instead chose to focus their attention and energy and that of the professional learning community on the potential implication of students not meeting goals. Rejecting the punishment portion of the accountability policies as a motivator, instructional leaders chose instead to consider how the policies and their performance targets informed what preparing students for their future truly meant.

Performance Evaluation Policy

As a mechanism for influencing professional practice, educational policies that provide guidance and regulatory pressure over performance evalu-ations have the ability to either support or provide a barrier to the development of a holistic practice of instructional leadership. Prior to the standards-based reform movement of the 1990s the performance evaluation of all educators was governed at state and local levels. The earliest part of the 21st century began a shift in the connection between federal education policy and educator performance evaluation through the use of school wide sanctions that included the removal of teachers and principals. Although not formally in their performance evaluation, the inclusion of job loss as a sanction linked state test scores to employment. It was the beginning of the second decade of the century that started a new chapter in educator evaluation with the federal government for the first time explicitly including elements and requirements of performance evaluations for educators in educational policy. The Elementary and Secondary Education Act (ESEA) flexibility waivers of 2012 provided states with the release of particular requirements of NCLB (2001) if they submit applications that articulated how they would ensure all students exited high school college and career ready, develop differentiated systems of accountability and support for educators, support the development of effective instructional and leadership practices, and reduce duplication of unnecessary burden (USDOE, 2012). Specifically through the development of effective practices, states were required to address educator evaluation. The expectation in the developed evaluation systems was that they include multiple measures of performance and that student growth on state assessments be considered a significant factor (Delisle, 2014). Stating that "strong evaluation and support systems guide teachers and principals in their work, provide more meaningful information about their effectiveness, and are useful for informing professional development, improving practices, and recognizing excellence," Secretary Delisle's letter to State Education Association leaders underscored the influence of federal policy on professional practices.

At the federal level the ESEA waiver policy required that the designed models:

1. Be used for continual improvement of instruction;
2. meaningfully differentiate performance using at least three performance levels;
3. use multiple valid measures in determining performance levels, including as a significant factor data on student growth for all students (including English Learners and students with disabilities), and other measures of professional practice (which may be gathered through multiple formats and sources, such as observations based on rigorous teacher performance standards, teacher portfolios, and student and parent surveys);
4. evaluate teachers and principals on a regular basis;

5. provide clear, timely, and useful feedback, including feedback that identifies needs and guides professional development; and
6. be used to inform personnel decisions.

(USDOE, 2012, p. 2)

Although including the requirement that evaluations must include multiple measures of performance including student growth, the policy language was somewhat broad and scant of guidance regarding the evaluation of principals, allowing State Educational Agencies to provide greater clarity and specificity about how evaluations would be conducted. In order to look more closely at the potential impact of the 2012 waivers on the professional practice of principals we'll look more closely at the implementation of the ESEA waivers through the context of the six New England States.

The New England Models

All but one of the New England states developed educator evaluation systems in response to seeking and being awarded a 2012 ESEA flexibility waiver. The remaining state, Vermont, developed a model independent of an ESEA waiver. While each of the models has their differences two key commonalities across the six states are the use of a set of either state determined or approved professional standards against which principals will be evaluated, and the use of either state determined or approved student learning data to determine some truth about the effectiveness of the professional practice of principals (CT DOE, 2012; MA DESE, 2013; Maine DOE, 2014; NH DOE, 2012; RI DOE, 2012; and VT DOE, 2012).

The use of student learning data to explicitly and formally make a statement about the effectiveness of principals is a new and developing element to the formal evaluation of the professional practice of school leaders. In each of the New England models the use of student learning data is handled differently with some states placing significant weight on student data and others providing a contextual application for the use of data. The models being implemented by the states of New Hampshire and Rhode Island place the most significant weight on student data as a measure of principal effectiveness by weighting student achievement data equally with assessment of professional practice when determining the effectiveness

Table 5.1 Weight of Student Learning Data in State Evaluation Models

State	Student Learning Data Points	Weight of Student Learning Data Points in Model
Connecticut (CT DOE, 2012)	Student growth on state administered assessments of core areas	Student Growth 22.5%
	At least two locally determined indicators of student learning, with at least one coming from subjects or grades not assessed through state system	Locally determined indicators 22.5%
Maine (ME DOE, 2013)	Student learning and growth measures	At least 20% of the educator's total score in the first year and 25% or more in subsequent years
Massachusetts (MA DOE, 2011)	Student growth percentile metric; locally determined measures of student achievement	Separate rating from performance; principals are rated as having low, medium, or high impact on student learning
New Hampshire (NH DOE, 2012)	Student growth measures	Equally weighted with assessment of professional practice
Vermont (VT DOE, 2012)	Student growth and learning outcomes encompassing classroom, school, district, and state assessments, as well as trends in growth scores (VT, DOE, 2012, p. 3)	Used as part of process of triangulating information gathered from observation and review of examination of artifacts
Rhode Island (RI DOE, 2013)	Student learning objective attainment and state growth model metric	Weighted equally with professional practice and foundations ratings

Source: Carrier, 2014

rating of principals. The implication is that student achievement is as much an indication of effective practice for principals as observed performance on the identified professional standards. At the opposite end of the spectrum Massachusetts utilizes assessment of student learning to essentially validate the performance rating of principals and Vermont is taking a more holistic approach by utilizing student learning data to triangulate the assessment of performance.

Each of the six New England state evaluation models meets the requirement for the inclusion of valid and reliable measures of student learning, each handles the use of this data differently. While the requirement that assessment of student learning produces valid and reliable data in order to be included in the evaluation models is important, as we think about how these policies define practice we must also consider the validity and reliability of the identified data for being an indicator of principal effectiveness. How can a measure of student achievement that was studied to ensure validity and reliability for determining student progress toward mastery of a defined set of curriculum standards also be a reliable and valid data source for determining the effectiveness of school principals? If a state places a great deal of weight on student achievement data in the evaluation process how might that affect the professional practice of principals?

As Hallinger and Heck noted in 1998 and as I found in 2011, principals may or may not have a direct influence on student achievement. As you'll remember from our discussion in Chapter 3 there is in truth no one right way to engage in the *work* of the principal and principals may be either directly or indirectly involved in the *work*. What makes a difference is if and how they engage in the practice of leadership. To that end, although a given evaluation model may overly weight student achievement data, caution is to be had that professional practice doesn't focus so much on short term solutions, work arounds, and other non-sustainable solutions to raising test scores that the inclusion of leadership in the practice of the principal is lost. Although the comparatively softer approach to utilizing student data being implemented in Massachusetts and Vermont to assess effectiveness would seem to place greater emphasis on the performance elements of the evaluation process, the questions of reliability and validity about the use of student achievement data, for this purpose facilitates keeping this element of the evaluation systems as a focal point for educators. We must be vigilant in asking, *how does the inclusion of this data impact my practice of instructional leadership?* Where does it place my focus and energy? Am I engaging in a holistic practice of instructional leadership or am I myopically engaged in the *work* elements of the model?

In an attempt to link student achievement data to professional performance, several of the states have included student learning objectives, commonly referred to as SLOs in their evaluation models. SLOs provide a useful tool for meaningfully linking student learning data to performance, but they do not fully satisfy the need to establish validity and reliability of student data as a measure for principal effectiveness. The argument can be made that a skilled and reflective evaluator could utilize a solid system of data inquiry to utilize student learning data as a tool for assessing the overall performance of principals and specifically the effectiveness with which they engage in their *work*. However, it would remain a challenge to assess the holistic practice of instructional leadership or more specifically to consider the leadership element of the practice.

Leadership behaviors, unlike technical skills, are often difficult to observe, identify, and capture leaving us with the issue of how to effectively assess leadership. In the context of instructional leadership we're more specifically left with the issue of how to assess the authentic and transformational leadership traits and behaviors that are necessary to having an effective practice. The use of stakeholder feedback in the evaluation of principals is a potential source of data for addressing this issue. Both Massachusetts and Connecticut have required stakeholder feedback as part of their evaluation models. While the Massachusetts stakeholder feedback only includes students and teachers, neither it nor the Connecticut model provides for the gathering of data relative to leadership behaviors. Void of a well-thought-out tool for gathering information about leadership behaviors, the process of collecting feedback from stakeholders for the purpose of formal evaluation is fraught with limitations to be identified and addressed.

Community Conformity

Coburn (2005) points out that the implementation of policies doesn't happen in isolation. It includes a complex system of other non-system players that influence the delivery and implementation of the policy in the field. That is, there isn't a direct line from policy developer to the schoolhouse that exists that is void of other influences. A key influencer of how we engage in our roles as schools leaders is the communities in which we work.

We all have mental models that dictate our paradigm for how we understand the world around us (Preskill & Torres, 1999). Our mental models are the sum total of our past experiences. They are based in the values of our families and communities. Popular media provides a mirror for us to consider our existing mental models. Whether meant to validate or challenge, we identify with the characters we see displayed on movie and television screens and in that way they influence and inform our existing mental models. As we consider our mental model of school principal who comes to mind? Is it Mr. Strickland from *Back to the Future* (Gale, Canton, & Zemeckis, 1985), Mr. Feeney from *Boy Meets World* (Jacobson, 1983–2000), Joe Clark from *Lean on Me* (Twain & Avidsen, 1989), *The Breakfast Club's* Mr. Vernon (Tanen & Hughes, 1985), or Rydell High's Principal McGee (Stigwood, Carr, & Kleiser, 1978) that you identify with in some way? When you first experienced these characters did they validate or challenge your mental model of the school principal? For most of us these satirical characterizations validated our experiences with school principals and in many ways prescribed our expectations for the role and perhaps even how we have engaged in it. But do these characters portray the role as it needs to be engaged in? Do they represent a disconnect between the expectations of the community for the role and our authentic selves?

The poem, *The Man in the Corner Office* captures the inner struggle that some leaders experience as they work through the gap between community expectations, mental models, and their authentic selves. Although gender biased, we can envision the woman in the corner office as well, dressed in her conservative business suit ensuring that everyone is doing what needs to be done. The desks may not be fancy and the chairs may or may not be leather but the principal's office is widely considered the seat of authority in a school. Teachers, students, and parents approach the office armed with the mental models of the principalship they have learned along the way. Too often their mental models have established the principal and their office is a place to avoid, a place to fear, and the place where directives are given and consequences doled out. As I entered into the role of principal this stereotyped model of the role was not what I endeavored into. It is not the role that my students envision as they draft their personal vision and mission statements but they can already see what I experienced getting in the way of making that vision for the role reality—community pressure.

Box 5.4 Voices from Leaders in the Field

Larry:

I see it with my parents that are less affluent in particular. They often didn't have great experiences with school themselves. Many have an idea that the principal's office is a place to avoid. If they come in I don't care if they have an appointment I want to see them, they are always welcome. I always take the time to speak with them. If I'm at dismissal or in the morning when the kids are coming in if I see them I make a point of talking to them. Not just about their kids, I do really try to highlight the good things, but about life in general. They need to see that I'm a real person too so they feel comfortable. I have one father that really had a hard time in school, he really likes cars and I like cars so whenever I get the chance I talk to him about cars. Now he comes into school to help out and to check in with his child's teachers. He just needed to know the office and the school weren't a bad place to be like when he was child.

Just as we have mental models for the role of the principal so do parents, the community at large, city councils, and school board members. While our mental models have been challenged and developed by virtue of our pursuit of education in the field of educational leadership and specifically in our pursuit to become licensed principals, the vast majority of the community members connected to our schools have not had that experience. They expect us to look, sound, and act like the principals they grew up with in school and in popular culture. While policy and moments of crisis may call for a change in how the role of the principal exists in schools, as Kevin Welner points out during school reform the instability of the system that occurs causes "a constant pressure to evolve toward the thing that existed before" (Zubrzycki, 2016). An often faced barrier to principals that seek to engage in a holistic model of instructional leadership is community pressure to conform to the predominant mental model of the role. The exemplar principals aren't cloistered behind closed doors waiting for the next appointment and doling out directives. They are not and don't seek to be feared or revered. These principals are actively and authentically

Box 5.5 Voices from Leaders in the Field

Lisa:

We do this end of the year family picnic—Multicultural night—everyone brings their food, and we do some other things. At first we had a hard time getting the Ukrainian parents to come. Gradually we made some inroads there. I realized the mothers that were here were looking at some of the Hispanic women that were up there dancing like crazy, just shocked, and some of the men. The men were even more worrisome. I realized the Russian women were afraid of the Hispanic men. Because they're big, many of them, and they had the do rags and the ear rings and the tattoos and ya know they looked like just kind of like rough guys. So we gradually began to bridge that gap by talking with the mothers [Russian and Ukrainian]. I first called in the mothers and wound up going to one of the houses, and I had to have a translator with me and we talked about it. They weren't saying too much and I said, "When you see those Spanish men, you're afraid of them, aren't you?" They all looked at each other and then one of them said, "How did you know?" I said, "Because I could see it on your faces; they're scary looking to you." That was an important conversation, we talked about cultural differences and slowly they started to come more and started to interact more.

engaged with the members of the school community; building positive, supportive, and trust-based relationships and engaging those around them in learning.

If we are to alter the mental models around us that exude pressure on our ability to engage in our roles as we envision them we must take responsibility for educating our communities. My first role in administration was that of a middle school assistant principal in an urban school. As I worked at making my vision for the role of school leader a reality I was purposeful about being out of my office and in classrooms observing learning. The byproduct of that was often a pile of discipline referrals that needed to be addressed during lunch and the entire afternoon. During a conversation with one of our veteran math teachers we discussed the volume of referrals and how quickly they would pile up while I was out in the classrooms. Her response both shocked me and confirmed my concerns about how the faculty perceived my role, "Well I don't know why you'd be out in classrooms anyway. You should be in the office issuing detentions and suspensions." I've never forgotten that exchange and have carried it with me as reminder that as an instructional leader it's my responsibility to educate others about my vision for the role and to support them in challenging and modifying their own mental models of the principalship.

Questions for Reflection and Discussion

1. Why did you want to become a school principal?
2. What is your personal vision?
3. What is your personal mission?
4. What elements of a holistic practice of instructional leadership does your state's evaluation model for principals support? Which does it appear to inhibit?
5. If your state's evaluation model appears to inhibit a holistic practice of instructional leadership what steps can you take to mitigate that influence on your practice?
6. Why has policy influenced your practice? What steps can you take to mitigate the effects?
7. How does your school community's expectation of the role of principal intersect with your vision for the role?
8. Now that you've identified your barriers what steps can you begin to take to overcome them?

References

Adams, J. L. (1993). Juggling job and family. *Vital Speeches of the Day,* 60(4), 125.

Carrier, L. (2011). *What is instructional leadership and what does it look like in practice? A multi-case case study of elementary school principals who have led schools from being identified as underperforming to performing.* Doctoral Dissertation. Boston, MA: University of Massachusetts.

Carrier, L. (2014). If we want to really improve our schools we need to make leadership a priority for instructional leaders. *The New Hampshire Journal of Education,* 17, 58–63.

Coburn, C. (2005). The role of nonsystem actors in the relationship between policy and practice: The case of reading instruction in California. *Educational Evaluation and Policy Analysis,* 27(1), 23–52.

Coburn, C., Hill, H., and Spillane, J. (2016). Alignment and accountability in policy design and implementation: The common core state standards and implementation research. *Educational Researcher,* 45(4), 243–251.

Connecticut State Department of Education (2012). *Connecticut guidelines for educator evaluation.* Retrieved on September 16, 2014 from www.sde.ct.gov/sde/lib/sde/pdf/rfp/connecticut_guidelines_for_educator_evaluation.pdf.

Delisle, D. (2014). *Letter to Chief State School Officers.* Retrieved on September 3, 2014 from www2.ed.gov/policy/eseaflex/secretary-letters/cssoltr8212014.html.

Fullan, M. (2001). *Leading in a Culture of Change.* San Francisco, CA: Jossey-Boss.

Gale, B. and Canton N. (Producers), Zemeckis, R., (Director) (1985). *Back to the Future.* United States: Universal Pictures.

Hallinger, P. and Heck, R. (1998). Exploring the principal's contribution to school effectiveness: 1980–1995. *School Effectiveness and School Improvement,* 9(2), 157–191.

Hargreaves, A. and Fink, D. (2006). *Sustainable Leadership.* San Francisco, CA: Jossey-Bass.

Jacobson, M. (Executive Producer) (1983–2000). *Boy Meets World.* Burbank, CA: Michael Jacobs Productions and Touchstone Television.

Jimerson, L. (2005). Placisim in NCLB—How rural children are left behind. *Equity and Excellence in Education,* 38(3), 211–219.

Maine Department of Education (2014). *State Principal Performance Evaluation and Professional Growth Models.* Retrieved on September 28, 2014 from http://maine.gov/doe/effectiveness/principals/index.html.

Massachusetts Department of Elementary and Secondary Education (2013). *Educator Evaluation*. Retrieved on September 5, 2014 from www.doe.mass.edu/edeval/.

New Hampshire Department of Education (2012). *New Hampshire ESEA flexibility: Request for window 3 (draft)*. Retrieved on September 10, 2014 from www.education.nh.gov/news/documents/flexibility-waiver-request.pdf.

No Child Left Behind Act (NCLB) (2001). P. L. 107–110, sec. 1116(b)(3). Retrieved on January 13, 2016 from www.nochildleftbehind.com/nclb-law-contents.html.

Preskill, H. and Torres, R.T. (1999). *Evaluative Inquiry for Learning in Organizations*. Thousand Oaks, CA: Sage Publications.

Rallis, S. and MacMullen, M. (2000). Inquiry-minded schools opening the doors for accountability. *Phi Delta Kappan*, June, 766–773.

Rhode Island Department of Education (2012). *Rhode Island model building administrator evaluation and support system*. Retrieved on September 23, 2014 from www.ride.ri.gov/TeachersAdministrators/EducatorEvaluation/GuidebooksForms.aspx.

Rossiter, C. (Ed.) (2014). The man in the corner office. *The Journal of Poetry Therapy*, 27(3), 155–156.

Spillane, J. (2006). *Distributed Leadership*. San Francisco, CA: Jossey-Bass.

Stigwood R., Carr, A. (Producers), and Kleiser, R. (Director) (1978). *Grease*. United States: Paramount Studios.

Tanen, N., Hughes, J. (Producers), and Hughes, J. (Director) (1985). *The Breakfast Club*. United States: Universal Pictures.

Twain, N. (Producer) and Avidsen, J. (Director) (1989). *Lean on Me*. United States: Warner Brothers.

United States Department of Education (2009). *The American recovery and reinvestment act of 2009: Saving and creating jobs and reforming education*. US Department of Education. Retrieved on September 16, 2009 from www2.ed.gov/policy/gen/leg/recovery/implementation.html.

United States Department of Education (2012). *Elementary and secondary education: ESEA flexibility*. Retrieved on September 1, 2014 from www2.ed.gov/policy/elsec/guid/esea-flexibility/index.html.

Vermont Department of Education (2012). *Vermont guidelines for teacher and leader effectiveness.* Retrieved on September 24, 2014 from http://education.vermont.gov/documents/EDU-Guidelines_for_Teacher_and_Leader_Effectiveness.pdf.

Zubrzycki, J. (2016, June 2). *Redesigned Denver School Gets Rocky Start. Education Week.* Retrieved on June 10, 2016 from www.edweek.org/ew/articles/2016/06/02/redesigned-denver-school-gets-rocky-start.html?qs=redesigned+denver+school.

6 | Keeping the Leadership in Your Practice

Richard Elmore (2000) identified instructional leadership as "the equivalent of the holy grail in educational administration" (p. 7). While on their quest to finding the grail many school leaders over the past twenty years have encountered perilous conditions that have left them confused and disoriented in their attempts to move forward. Amidst the variety of day to day demands of their jobs and external pressures of the k-12 educational system they've missed the cairns on the trail that marked key points in their journey to becoming an instructional leader. Hopefully, through our conversation over these pages you are now able to see the milestones in your own journey to a practice of holistic instructional leadership. It is my hope that you now see the places in your practice where you engage in the *work* of principals, where you engage in *leadership* behaviors, and how your leadership influences the effectiveness of the *work*. It's also my hope that your reflections have provided you with clarity over how to proceed on your personal quest.

While we each may find our way as individuals, the journey will be difficult if we continue to try and make it alone. In order to ease the continuing struggle on us each as individuals we must each act as leaders of our profession. As school leaders we continuously and passionately advocate for needed resources for our schools. Just as we advocate for financial and human resources we must also advocate for the resources to facilitate the development and support of effective practices; including our own. If we as school leaders are going to keep the leadership in instructional leadership we must become strong advocates for a holistic practice.

Advocating for Effective Practice

As we fearlessly advocate for our schools we must be clear about our practice of instructional leadership and how it impacts student achievement. As a resource for our schools we must advocate for it as well. What do we need in terms of support, professional development, and other resources to develop our practice into the holistic model of instructional leadership necessary to effectively lead schools? Educational policies, school district practices, principal preparation and professional development programs have substantial impact on the field but most often are focused on the *work* of principals, not the practice of leadership, and not the holistic practice of instructional leadership we have been discussing. In that way they become potential barriers to the development of a holistic practice, but these external influences can be moved toward becoming more consistent and effective networks of support. To make that a reality we each must take up the responsibility of educating the world outside our schools about the need for a holistic practice of instructional leadership and about our needs as professionals for resources that help us develop and sustain that practice.

What does being an advocate for an effective practice of instructional leadership mean? Many of us are members of state, regional, and national professional organizations. Those of us that are members proudly add our membership to resumes and other materials. We are proud members of these organizations. We show our support through our membership dues, sharing that we're members, and perhaps we attend the annual conference, but what does membership really mean? How does our membership establish us as advocates for the profession we are so deeply committed to? While membership is important and provides us with access to a variety of professional development resources it does not establish us as advocates if we are not actively engaged with and in the organization. Obviously it's not possible for everyone to be on the committees of professional organizations but we can each be a voice for what an effective holistic practice of instructional leadership is and what we need from the organization as a professional to make that a reality. As advocates for practice it's imperative that we actively communicate our professional needs to organization leadership.

For the vast majority of us our personal circle of influence for advocating for practice includes our school district leaders, policy-makers, professional development providers, and local institutes of higher education. Members of each of these organizations identify with us as individuals and professionals and it is through our relationship with them we are able to become strong advocates for our profession.

Developing District Level Support for Instructional Leadership

Over the course of these pages you've been developing a vision for your professional practice. You've considered the elements of the *work* of principals and how you'll ensure those happen in your practice. Likewise you've considered the *leadership* of principals and how you'll include that in your practice. Finally, you've considered how you can use *leadership* to make the *work* of principals more effective in your school. But who will you communicate your vision with and what will you communicate about it?

Begin by communicating your new vision with other educational leaders in your school. As we've discussed, as instructional leaders we are focused on learning and must model that for those we lead. By sharing our developing vision for practice we not only do that but we begin to engage those we lead in the learning process as well. Together as a professional learning group (PLG) you can discuss, process, and analyze current school practices; and together create a plan to develop current instructional leadership practices in the school to a more holistic model. As the conversation continues, together you can delve deeply into your practices and develop a holistic practice that best meets the needs of your school and community.

Once you've further developed your vision through your work with your school PLG it's important to communicate your developing vision, and the developing vision of your PLG, with your immediate supervisor and with your superintendent if s/he is not that person. They will be the ones that will need to assist you with support for development and sustainability of a holistic practice. They will also be the ones to support you in elevating the conversation about practice to a district wide level. By engaging in collegial conversation with district level leaders about how we're trying to develop our professional practice and it's possible to not only influence our own practice but the practices of the district. Two school district oriented structures that can provide substantial impact for the development and sustainability of a holistic practice of instructional leadership are mentoring/coaching and induction programs.

The concept of providing induction, mentoring, and instructional coaching for teachers is a common and widely accepted group of professional development practices in the pk-12 public school system. For most

> ### Box 6.1 Voices from Leaders in the Field
>
> *Doug:*
>
> When I started, when you got a mentor it was usually somebody retired, who was probably a friend of the superintendent. It was somebody who had worked in the district and was extremely well intentioned. You know usually they had a lot of time on their hands, and they loved going out to lunch and going to a lot of meetings and it was great. It was very nice. It was kind of one of those mentor things. But when I was in graduate school one of my best courses was cognitive coaching and it was totally new to me, but my mom was a marriage, family, child counselor and so I kind of understood creating conversations where people were not giving advice but were creating a way to give themselves advice. They were able to create their own solutions . . . so that's all part of it for me and how I've worked with teachers.
>
> Because of that I'm really interested in taking the same conversations I had with teachers and having them with principals so I became a principal mentor through NAESP. I always wanted someone who's still practicing to be able to talk to me. Somebody who's 10 years in, 5 years in, 15 years in and there wasn't anyone who could give that kind of opportunity around here. And we were given the opportunity through our State Principals Association to go through the mentor training and I wanted to see if that was something that could kind of bridge that gap of being a principal and then talking with other principals . And what I found was that I learned more than the people I worked with because it gave me the ability to look inside their world and see what their thinking was and learn "oh, ok they're handling that situation in that way. I don't have that situation here, that's interesting."

of us as school leaders the idea of those practices as sources of professional development is less common. This is further evidenced through a recent ERIC data base search, which gleaned thirty-eight articles written on the topic of school principals and induction, mentoring, or coaching between the years 2010 and 2015. Looking more deeply at the articles, only thirteen actually addressed principals as the inductee, mentee, or professional being coached. Only six of the articles were subjected to the peer review process, suggesting scant empirical research on the topic. This stands in stark contrast to the 769 articles written, of which 485 were peer reviewed, during the same time period on teacher induction, mentoring and coaching programs.

Although little is known about the practices at local levels, state-wide programs like the Kansas Educational Leadership Institute (KELI) have shown promising results with providing wide scale induction, mentoring, and coaching. Through the provision of opportunities for deep learning about issues of practice, and onsite mentoring and coaching from veteran school leaders KELI participants were able to develop their knowledge of the elements of the *work* of principals while developing the *leadership* their school and community requires (Augustine-Shaw, 2016). The lessons learned from KELI have the potential to be scaled to regional and district level programs. To do so however will require that we each act as advocates for our profession.

Educating and Working with Policy-Makers

Parents and all members of the community have the potential to influence local, state, and federal educational policy decisions through their financial and political support of decisions, initiatives, and policies. One only need look at the impact of the *Opt Out* movement of recent years, for evidence of their influence (Disare, 2016; Harris & Fessenden, 2015; Skinner, 2016). The impact of this controversial movement has resulted in state statutes that provide for parent opt-out of state testing without negative consequences for students, shifts in testing requirements (NH DOE, 2015), and political debate during the 2016 election cycle regarding elimination of the Common Core State Standards. Through educating parents and the community about educational testing, activist groups like The National Center for Fair and Open Testing and NYS Allies for Public Education were able to leverage the political power of parents and the community to effect change. Just as it is our role and responsibility as instructional leaders to focus on learning in our schools, as advocates for our professional practice it's also our responsibility to focus on learning as it pertains to parents and the community at large. As advocates for our profession we must educate the community on the difference between school management and leadership, the need for a holistic practice of instructional leadership, and what we need in order to make that a reality.

In addition to parents and other constituents in our school's community it's our responsibility as educational leaders to build relationships with our local, state, and federal legislatures in order to engage them in conversation about the needs of our students, schools, and profession. Policy-makers are commonly invited into schools to read to students or to speak to them about government, and as advocates of the profession we must take these opportunities to engage these policy-makers in the conversation. We must educate them about the influence of policy on practice, the difference between management and leadership, and why a holistic practice of instructional leadership is necessary. We must also educate them on what we need as a profession in order to have the capacity to develop and sustain that type of practice. By developing strong relationships with our state and federal policy-makers we can engage them as partners in the development of educational policies that support our efforts to develop our practice rather than become barriers to them.

Working with Institutes of Higher Education and Professional Development Providers

In 1996, the Council for Chief State School Officers (CCSSO) released the Interstate School Leaders Licensure Consortium (ISLLC) professional standards for the training and performance development of school leaders. Since that time the majority of states have connected their professional licensure requirements and evaluation systems to that set of standards. In 2007, Carla Toye and her colleagues reported that forty-three states were either directly using the standards, using a modified version, or had aligned their professional standards for principals to the ISLLC standards. Subsequently, the majority of principal training programs in the United States base their curriculum on those standards.

Although the demands in the field of education have changed since 1996, the professional standards guiding the training and professional development of school principals did not until 2015. In response to the changing demands on the roles of school leaders, the National Policy Board for Educational Administration (NPBEA) in collaboration with CCSSO developed and released a new set of professional standards (NPBEA, 2015). The Professional Standards for Educational Leaders (PSEL) replaced ISLLC and provide a refreshed view of the role of school principal in the 21st century. Acknowledging a recognition of the "central importance of human relationships" (NPBEA, 2015, p. 3), there is hope that the new standards will provide support for the delineation of management and leadership behaviors in the practice of principals.

While a common set of standards exists, much like the curriculum standards we implement with our pk-12 students, there is a vast amount of discrepancy around the types of educational experiences students are exposed to and what mastery of the standards looks like. Although the majority of programs include some kind of field experience work or internship experience, these experiences often fail to bridge the theory to practice gap. Candidates are often, but not always, granted limited release time from their regular assignments, allowing them little time to engage in the real issues of school. Additionally, because candidates are typically still employed in their regular job assignments, they most often conduct their field and internship experiences in their schools, potentially not working under the guidance of a mentor that is skilled in the holistic practice of instructional leadership. This was made apparent to me during an initial site visit with one of my practicum students. During the visit the mentor, student, and I spoke about the requirements for the practicum and the types of experiences the students should engage in. At the conclusion of our conversation the mentor, who was the building principal and very veteran in his role, looked at the two of us and said, "I don't know how to do any of these things. I do discipline. But you tell me what you need and I'll make sure you are able to do it." I had great admiration for his honesty but deep concern for him as professional and for us as a profession.

The question becomes what can we as a profession do about it? By engaging with institutions of higher education and professional development providers about our learning needs we can begin to influence the pre-service and in-service learning opportunities these agencies provide. How are they defining instructional leadership? Are they working from a holistic view point of the construct or are they focused on one piece of it? Are they able to offer field and internship experiences that are meaningful and with field mentors that are skilled in the practice of holistic leadership? Are they supporting mentors in the development of their own practice and in their guidance of candidates? Perhaps most importantly, as a professional in our field how can you and your PLG work with your local principal licensure programs to help them move toward programs that effectively support students in bridging the gap from theory to practice?

Pausing the Conversation

Over the course of this book we've considered our practice as instructional leaders deeply. Hopefully, you have begun to develop your vision and have begun to think about how to move forward with it. I'm also hopeful that you have begun to think about how you can be a leader for our profession. I encourage you not to end the conversation but to pause it and continue it beyond the chapters of this book. The conversation about the holistic practice of instructional leadership needs to continue beyond a single book, conference, workshop, or research study if we are to truly move forward as a profession. We must all as members of our profession take responsibility for ensuring that's the case. Likewise, we all as instructional leaders need to choose the road on which we will continue our personal journeys to becoming holistic instructional leaders. We must each continue our journey intentionally with a plan for navigating difficult terrain and with a map of the milestones we'll seek along the way.

Questions for Reflection and Discussion

1. How will you engage other leaders in your school in the conversation about developing a holistic practice of instructional leadership?
2. How will you engage your school district's leadership in the conversation about developing a holistic practice of instructional leadership?
3. Who are the local, state, and federal policy-makers for your school community? How will you engage them in the conversation about developing a holistic practice of instructional leadership?

4. Who are the professional development providers and higher education programs that support pre-service and in-service training of principals? How will you engage them in the conversation about developing a holistic practice of instructional leadership?

5. As you develop your own practice, how will you manage potential barriers to your progress?

6. As you develop your own practice what benchmarks will you accept as evidence of your progress?

References

Augustine-Shaw, D. (2016). Developing Leadership Capacity in New Rural School District Leaders: The Kansas Educational Leadership Institute. *The Rural Educator, 37*(1), 1–13.

Disare, M., (2016). *New York's opt-out movement aims to influence policy, not just parents. Here's how.* Retrieved on June 1, 2016 http://www.chalkbeat.org/posts/ny/2016/02/05/new-yorks-opt-out-movement-aims-to-influence-policy-not-just-parents-heres-how/.

Elmore, R. (2000). *Building a New Structure for School Leadership.* Washington, DC: Albert Shanker Institute.

Harris, E. and Fessenden, F. (2015). *Opt Out' Becomes Anti-Test Rallying Cry in New York State.* Retrieved on June 1, 2016 from www.nytimes.com/2015/05/21/nyregion/opt-out-movement-against-common-core-testing-grows-in-new-york-state.html?_r=0.

National Policy Board for Educational Administration (2015). *Professional Standards for Educational Leaders 2015.* Reston, VA: Author.

New Hampshire Department of Education (2015). *New Hampshire ESEA Flexiblity Renewal Request.* Retrieved on June 15, 2016 from http://education.nh.gov/accountability-system/documents/flexibility-waiver-request-renewal.pdf.

Skinner, V. (2016). *Florida parents sue state after third-graders held back for opting out of standardized test.* Retrieved on August 20, 2016 from http://eagnews.org/florida-parents-sue-state-after-third-graders-held-back-for-opting-out-of-standardized-test/.

Toye, C., Blank, R., Sanders, N. M., & Williams, A. (2007). *Key State Education Policies on P-12 Education: 2006. Results of a 50 state survey.* Washington, DC: Council of Chief State School Officers.

Taylor & Francis eBooks

Helping you to choose the right eBooks for your Library

Add Routledge titles to your library's digital collection today. Taylor and Francis ebooks contains over 50,000 titles in the Humanities, Social Sciences, Behavioural Sciences, Built Environment and Law.

Choose from a range of subject packages or create your own!

Benefits for you
- Free MARC records
- COUNTER-compliant usage statistics
- Flexible purchase and pricing options
- All titles DRM-free.

Benefits for your user
- Off-site, anytime access via Athens or referring URL
- Print or copy pages or chapters
- Full content search
- Bookmark, highlight and annotate text
- Access to thousands of pages of quality research at the click of a button.

REQUEST YOUR FREE INSTITUTIONAL TRIAL TODAY

Free Trials Available
We offer free trials to qualifying academic, corporate and government customers.

eCollections – Choose from over 30 subject eCollections, including:

Archaeology	Language Learning
Architecture	Law
Asian Studies	Literature
Business & Management	Media & Communication
Classical Studies	Middle East Studies
Construction	Music
Creative & Media Arts	Philosophy
Criminology & Criminal Justice	Planning
Economics	Politics
Education	Psychology & Mental Health
Energy	Religion
Engineering	Security
English Language & Linguistics	Social Work
Environment & Sustainability	Sociology
Geography	Sport
Health Studies	Theatre & Performance
History	Tourism, Hospitality & Events

For more information, pricing enquiries or to order a free trial, please contact your local sales team:
www.tandfebooks.com/page/sales

The home of Routledge books

www.tandfebooks.com